MW00613676

"Sam and Nasutsa ta
tomer focused approach in their explanation of the impacts
of fire and water damage.

Every day, thousands of people are affected by the devastating
results from fire and water damages in their lives. This book
helps explain the steps involved in the restoration process.
Keeping in mind that while the process is very technical
and is impacted by a multitude of variables. The customer
doesn't need to know how to build a watch to understand
time, nor do they need to understand psychrometry when a
restoration company is drying their home. They put their trust
in the process and this book will help explain and walk them
through those many steps.

I've worked in the industry for over 37 years, owning and
managing restoration and cleaning businesses and training
other restoration professionals to serve customers. Sam and
Nasutsa take these skills to new levels and help others see
what a professional can be."

Pete Duncanson, CMRS, MWR, WFR, MTC,
Past Chairman of the Board for the IICRC
Approved IICRC instructor

Sam Simon + Nasutsa Mabwa

Copyright© 2022, Restoration By Simons

All rights reserved.

No portion of this book may be reproduced by mechanical, photographic or electronic process, nor may it be stored in a retrieval system, transmitted in any form or otherwise be copied for public use or private use without written permission of the Copyright Owner.

It is sold with the understanding that the publisher and the individual authors are not engaged in the rendering of psychological, legal, accounting or other professional advice. The content and views in each chapter are the sole expression and opinion of its author and not necessarily the views of Fig Factor Media, LLC.

For more information, contact:
Fig Factor Media | www.figfactormedia.com

Cover Design by Marco Alvarez
Layout by LDG Juan Manuel Serna Rosales

Printed in the United States of America

ISBN: 978-1-952779-52-7

Library of Congress Control Number: 2022904674

Restore

A complete guide to protecting
your home as your most valuable
asset from water and fire disasters

Sam Simon + Nasutsa Mabwa

TABLE OF CONTENTS

Our mission v

Introduction viii

Part 1: WATER...1

1. Is Your Water Damage New or Old? 3
2. When DIY Is Not a Good Idea 5
3. Why Only Professionals Should Tackle Raw Sewage Cleanup 7
4. What to Do If You Have a Sewer Backup....................9
5. Seven Negative Effects of Water Damage In Your Home 18
6. How a Disaster May Add Value to Your Property.......21
7. How to Restore Items after They've Been Water Damaged..23
8. How Hidden Water Damage Can Affect Your Home . 27
9. How to Shield Your Home from Moisture and Humidity 29
10. What to Do If I've Got a Faulty Waterline...................32
11. The Three Warning Signs Indicating a Broken Pipe .. 34
12. Why Pipes Freeze and How to Stop It From Happening to You 36
13. What to Do About Frozen and Burst Pipes.................38
14. How to Winterize Your Home.....................................45
15. How to Avoid Water Damage From Your Water Heater 48
16. How to Avoid Water Damage While on Vacation 50
17. What Can Happen If You Ignore Water Damage In Your Home 53
18. Three Reasons Why Your Roof Is Leaking 56

19. What Should I Do If My Wood Floors Are Wet: An Ultimate Guide..59

20. Top Tips for Preventing Basement Seepage 63

21. How to Prevent Ice Dams..66

Part 2: FIRE 71

1. Residential Fire Damage 101: What Do I Do If There's a Fire in My Home?...73

2. What Is Fire Content Cleaning?...............................77

3. What to Do If Caught in a House Fire........................81

4. How to Keep Your Appliances from Going up in Smoke 83

5. How to Prevent Puff Backs in Your Home 87

6. Holiday Fire Prevention 89

7. Avoid Fire Damage From Holiday Lights and Decorations 91

8. After a Fire in Your Home: What to Save, What to Toss..93

9. Eight Fire Safety Tips for People with Disabilities 95

10. Fire Dangers Don't End When the Flames Are Dowsed 97

11. Fire Extinguisher Safety Tips that Can Save Your Life 100

12. Don't Be a Victim of Carbon Monoxide Poisoning ...102

13. Lingering Tobacco Odors Are Still a Health Hazard.. 105

14. Grill Safety 108

15. Use Extension Cords Safely to Prevent the Need for Fire Restoration 110

16. Hoarding Greatly Increases the Risk of Fire Damage... 112

Part 3: INSURANCE **115**

1. The Most Common Causes of Property Damage for Homeowners 117

2. How to Read Your Homeowners Insurance Policy... 119

3. Five Things Not Covered by Homeowners Insurance... 122

4. Thirteen Surprising Things You May Not Know You are Covered for.. 125

5. Common Factors Affecting Your Insurance Rate..... 132

6. Five Things You Need to Ask Your Insurance Agent 133

7. Homeowners Insurance vs Renters Insurance 135

8. Flood Insurance.. 138

9. Five Tips for Choosing Home Insurance 140

Part 4: CLEANING & DISINFECTION.............................. 143

1. Can You Clean with Only Water? 145

2. Tips for Making Your Home Look and Smell Spring Clean 149

3. When Chemicals and Extreme Temperatures Don't Mix.. 152

4. Does Your Renovation Budget Include Post Construction Cleaning Costs?................................... 154

5. Biohazard Cleanup – What, When and Why? 158

6. Home Ventilation: How Ventilation Prevents the Spread of Viruses Indoors.. 160

7. How HEPA Filters Protect You 164

8. Is Bleach a Safe Disinfectant?................................ 166

9. Should Green Cleaning Products Be Used to Disinfect? 171

10. Why Hoarding Cleanup Should Only Be Done by Professionals 173

11. What Cold Weather Means for Viruses.................... 176

About the authors 179

Acknowledgements.. 183

OUR MISSION

Our mission at Restoration By Simons is to provide the best fire and water damage restoration and specialty cleaning services to our customers. Our aim is to restore calm amidst the chaos that can result from a disaster to residential and commercial properties.

As leaders at the forefront of recovery, restoration and decontamination services, we have a hands-on approach with all of our customers. We want to educate and empower you so you can make sound decisions when it comes to the cleaning and restoration of your properties.

We provide up-front personal service and support, as customer satisfaction is our number one goal. This is achieved by valuing and empowering our team of project managers, technicians, and office staff.

As a minority, woman-owned and family-operated firm, we highly value diversity, social justice, racial equity and ethics and instill these essential values throughout the company.

About Restoration By Simons

As an Institute of Inspection Cleaning and Restoration Certification (IIRC) Certified Firm, Restoration By Simons follows IICRC S500 Standards for professional water damage restoration. Our IICRC certified technicians will assess the water damage on-site and determine the best course of action to restore your damaged property. For example, clean water damage from a faulty waterline pipe on your property is considerably different from water damage from a sewer backup. As leading experts in the field, we will quickly determine the best course of action so your family or business can get back to normal as soon as possible. Professional restoration companies such as Restoration By Simons have IICRC trained technicians, appropriate equipment and the experience necessary for a quick and efficient intervention.

Restoration By Simons MBE/WBE certified firm and family-run company located in the Chicagoland area. Recently, the company was awarded a variety of honors, including is a SB100 Best of Small Business Award Winner 2021, Bronze Stevie® Award in the Female Entrepreneur of the Year category in the 18th annual Stevie Awards for Women in Business, recipient of the 2020 Better Business Bureau's Torch Award for Marketplace Ethics, and recipient of the 2020 Skokie Business of the Year Award, Honorable Mention Category.

Restoration By Simons provides disaster restoration services including water and flood damage restoration, fire and smoke damage restoration, mold remediation and a wide range of interior specialty cleaning, including hoarder and clutter cleaning, post-construction cleaning, carpet cleaning and upholstery cleaning to residential and commercial customers. For more information, give us a call at 773-376-1110 or visit restorationbysimons.com to learn more about our services.

- https://restorationbysimons.com/
- https://www.facebook.com/restorationbysimons
- https://www.linkedin.com/company/2997771/
- https://www.youtube.com/channel/ UCINZ1MuPJRt05NuwwPcxFcw

INTRODUCTION

We first met as social workers in the mid 90's in Chicago's Wicker Park neighborhood.

Social work was challenging, emotionally rewarding and introduced us to many different types of people from all over the city. We worked with families and provided a myriad of support in many ways. Our social work experience has become the communicative foundation we rely on today in our work with customers of the restoration company we founded in 2012.

So how did we end up running a disaster restoration company? It has been a long voyage full of twists and turns along the way. We both had successful careers in our respective fields. Nasutsa was an executive in commercial real estate development and Sam worked in national television production. Our individual successes came from hard work, which often meant long hours on the job. As we started our family, we realized that we wanted to be more available to our children, which was an issue, since both of our jobs provided no opportunity for working from home. We talked about starting our own business. We thought about buying and flipping properties, which we actually did for several years. We started an urban landscape design business which didn't quite turn out the way we'd hoped and didn't pay very well either. Then we decided to start a fast-casual street food restaurant. The concept was novel and no one yet had brought this concept to Chicago. We designed the menus, found a location in Chicago's Wicker Park that worked for us. We had $125,000 startup money from a small neighborhood bank near the restaurant's location. Then, just one day later, fate intervened.

An acquaintance who owned a restoration franchise was telling Sam about his business, his struggles and successes, and his happiness in both his personal and professional life as a restoration owner. We were intrigued. He invited Sam on board as a junior partner and we scrapped our plans for the restaurant, setting off on a journey that would eventually lead us to be owners of our own company.

Our company, Restoration By Simons, is a minority, woman and family-owned local business providing disaster restoration and specialty cleaning services to residential and commercial customers throughout the Chicago metropolitan area.

Over the years, we've gained a lot of useful and important first-hand knowledge on how to restore homes and businesses following a wide range of disasters. We've worked on thousands of projects with the end goal in mind to help our customers through disruptive and stressful emergencies. During these projects, we genuinely help and support our customers while providing a positive experience.

By imparting useful information and tips out of habit, and acting as a key resource whenever possible, we are the go-to when it comes to complicated restoration projects. Thus, the book you are holding in your hands. Our company has handled difficult restoration projects for both residential and commercial customers, ranging from water damage to flooding, fire damage to mold remediation, hoarder clean ups to cleaning and disinfection during a pandemic. Through our work we've learned new practical skill sets and amassed a wide range of information about how to approach all sorts of restoration projects as a hands-on service provider. This book can be read from cover to cover, or in sections, shared as a reference guide, or for group lunch and learn sessions. This resource is our way of sharing helpful and important information with you. We would also like our readers to know that this book should be used as a guide and not everything written in this book is applicable to everyone in all circumstances. Your unique situation may require a different approach best determined by the restoration professional you choose to work with.

We truly hope that you find something of value within these pages. Even better, perhaps you could pass on things you've learned to others. That, to us, is how we can all restore a little more peace, a little more positivity into the world.

Sincerely, your restoration partners,
Authors Sam Simon & Nasutsa Mabwa

PART 1:

WATER

———

Water damage can happen at any time and be a minimal or a major disruption to your property. For example, you may be out of town and your fifty-gallon water boiler leaks throughout the basement, or it's wintertime, a frozen pipe bursts on the second floor of your home, cascading water down through the home, damaging your contents and furniture, and the structure along the way. There are many situations where water mitigation and water restoration services may be needed.

The response time in which a water damage restoration company reacts is essential. The faster we can arrive on-site, the shorter drying time, meaning less costs to you and your insurance.

The most devastating of natural disasters—such as a flood—happen without warning. Other unfortunate events, like pipe bursts, leaking water heaters and other plumbing mishaps, also occur when least expected, but leave behind a similar amount of water damage and devastation. We understand that for property owners, experiencing water damage can be difficult and stressful. In addition, damage caused by water can increase substantially if not addressed promptly. Our restoration process includes fast, competent water damage cleanup. We are typically on-site as soon as possible to halt further damage and remove water and moisture. After that, we work to restore your home to its former condition.

1. Is Your Water Damage New or Old?

Water damage is the most frequent form of property damage due to the many ways it can occur. Nature may be the culprit as rainstorms and flooding can lead to water damage, but it can also happen when pipes burst or when sewage backups let water flow into your residential or commercial property, damaging it in the process.

But sometimes the damage may be hidden, so you might not spot it right away. Once you do, you may wonder about just how long ago the damage occurred. As time goes by, water damage that hasn't been remediated will start deteriorating its surroundings and cause more harm. So knowing when a particular area has experienced water damage can help to give you an idea as to the degree of damage as well as the importance of having the damage restored.

If you notice that water damage has occurred but aren't sure when it happened, use the following tips to determine whether it's new or old.

Touch the affected area

Fresh water damage will still be moist, but the impacted material will still be firm, not soft. Older water damage will create soft, mushy spots because of the longer amount of time the material has been affected by moisture.

For example, drywall that's experienced a new water damage will be damp but still stable. It will still have its structural integrity because the water hasn't had time to do much harm. Drywall with older water damage, however, will have a softer consistency since more time has gone by, allowing water to absorb into and damage the drywall. To help you work out how long drywall has been wet, here's an important fact: standing water can wick up drywall at a rate of one inch per hour for the first 24 hours.

Look for rings

Staining is one of the common signs of water damage. More precisely, rings may develop on softer materials, such as drywall, when they've been damaged by water. If you notice a dark spot without any rings around it, this indicates that the water damage is new. Older, periodic water damage (for example, a slow leak) will have rings around it, and much like a tree, the more rings, the older the damage. Different shades of rings show that the area has been soaked, dried, soaked, dried, etc.

Search for mold growth

Water damage and mold growth go together like bacon and eggs because water damage produces the perfect conditions for mold spores to grow and form colonies. Mold needs both moisture and a food source (cellulose-based materials such as wood, cardboard, paper, drywall, etc.) to grow. When mold spores encounter both, this activates mold growth. Mold damages materials it grows on. In fact, mold damage can get so bad that it adversely affects a building's structural integrity.

So, if you come across mold growing in your home,

there's a good chance that water damage has happened somewhere in the structure. Mold develops within 24-48 hours of water exposure and will continue growing until the source of moisture is removed.

2. When DIY Is Not a Good Idea

DIY, or Do it Yourself, isn't new. People have been DIY-ing since, well, forever. In recent years, the growth of the DIY industry has exploded, thanks to the popularity of an endless variety of TV shows on networks like DIY and HGTV. But when they're not watched with a practical eye, shows that complete their projects in thirty minutes to an hour can trick people into thinking their project will also be easy.

For instance, some people attempt to save money on the expense of water or mold damage restoration by skipping the process of hiring restoration professionals. Instead, they try to handle the tear-out and dry-out processes themselves. For many "minor" spills (those only involving a few gallons of water at most), this can be fine as long as the spill is cleaned up quickly and occurs well away from walls or other places where the moisture from the spill can reach a gap and seep into the subfloor. But for more serious water damage scenarios, DIY is usually NAGI (not a good idea).

Whenever there's a major amount of moisture damage, it's very important for a professional restoration service to be brought in to manage the dry-out process. Without the help of a trained and experienced expert, someone who attempts DIY moisture removal may miss pockets of moisture in the building, leading to:

Damaged building infrastructure

Moisture can seep into the structural materials behind the walls and under the floor, causing damage. But with proper dry-out and moisture remediation, much of the damage can be mitigated or even avoided.

Warped flooring

When moisture seeps into subfloor materials, it can cause wooden boards to shift, bend and cup. This creates an uneven floor and poses a safety risk to the building's occupants. If they're salvageable, only professional restoration equipment can return them to normal.

Mold growth

Left unchecked, moisture trapped in a building can promote the growth of mold, particularly in cool, dark places such as basements and in-between walls. As any IAQ (Indoor Air Quality) Specialist can tell you, mold spores in the air pose a serious respiratory risk to children and people with respiratory conditions such as asthma.

As a rule of thumb, if the water or mold damage to your home is severe enough to warrant an insurance claim, then you shouldn't try to handle the restoration process on your own. Damage that occurs as a result of DIY restoration efforts is typically not covered by insurance. Furthermore, restoration work can be hazardous for those who haven't been trained for the risks associated with working with dirty water, mold and water-damaged structures.

3. Why Only Professionals Should Tackle Raw Sewage Cleanup

Whether you've smelled it as you've driven by a spill or you've had it backed up in your home, the nauseating odor of raw sewage is difficult to forget. Sadly, the terrible odor isn't the worst of it.

What is raw sewage?

Raw sewage is waste that has not been cleaned and treated and originates from residential, institutional or business buildings. It isn't simply liquid; it may also contain toilet paper, feminine hygiene products and additional human wastes. It's also called black water, which is swarming with deadly bacteria and viruses that can turn previously clean and safe indoor living areas into contaminated danger zones.

What are the health risks?

Raw sewage is a mixture of foul material. It's the perfect breeding ground for nearly all kinds of bacteria, viruses and microorganisms. Raw sewage consists of an almost endless list of toxic pathogens and contact with them can cause you to be violently ill or perhaps kill you.

How do professionals protect themselves?

It's vital that raw sewage is kept from touching your skin, especially where there are cuts, sores and any mucus membrane related to the eyes, ears and nose. That's why disaster restoration professionals cover up entirely in PPE (personal protective equipment) which involves full body suits, full face respirators, gloves, rubber boots, etc. They additionally keep a complete stock of respirator and sanitizer wipes, as well as access to an eye-wash station and a change of clothes.

What can I do to protect my family?

Keep animals, kids and the elderly away from the area that's been contaminated as they're typically more vulnerable to germs and bacteria. Carefully wash all items touched by sewage immediately. Though it's not always possible to avoid raw sewage backups, you can decrease the odds of one happening by having your drain lines examined at least twice annually. Also, make sure you repair slow drains immediately, don't pour grease down drains and have your pipes flushed frequently.

Can sewage damaged contents be saved?

If some contents of your home were soiled by sewage, your first thought might be to quickly dispose of them. But though they may have been saturated in the worst sludge imaginable, many can be meticulously cleaned and sanitized so that you can securely use them again. But there are exceptions:

- Absorbent materials or items that soaked up any sewage water are non-salvageable and must be discarded. These include carpeting and padding, mattresses, upholstered furniture, curtains, books, etc. Clothes, towels, and linens can generally be safely laundered and disinfected.

- Porous structural objects such as saturated drywall, baseboard trim, paneling, insulation, and comparable materials that have absorbed wastewater cannot be disinfected and also have to be removed. If black water has seeped below the flooring, the flooring material might also need removal.

If you have questions about whether some of the contents in your home are salvageable or not, contact a professional that has the experience, equipment and disinfectants needed to safely clean them up, protecting you and your family from becoming deathly ill.

4. What to Do If You Have a Sewer Backup?

Sewer backups are a real pain! The unexpected event can cause a significant amount of stress and disruption on your property if not properly cared for — plus dealing with it prevents you from attending to other important matters.

What is a "sewer backup?"
Sewer backups occur during periods of heavy rainfall and when your city's sewer system can no longer handle the excess water, causing it to overflow into your property. This water emerges from your plumbing and can wreak havoc on your properties, especially on lower floors. It also usually

smells really bad! The most serious backups happen on the main sewer line, which is the single common pipe that all of your drains eventually lead to. It is also the pipe that delivers that wastewater to the main municipal sewer line or a private septic tank. If your clog or blockage is on the main sewer line, it's not safe to run any water in your property or flush your toilets when sewer backups occur because there's nowhere for that waste to escape to. Often, the first signs of a blockage in a sewer line are drains that will not work properly and gurgling toilets. This can even sometimes sound like your toilet is percolating.

Human activity can also cause a clog or backup on a single drain line. This typically happens when people rinse large food scraps and grease down a sink, or when something out of the norm is flushed down the toilet. These backups or clogs can sometimes be resolved with a smaller tool, like a toilet auger or drain snake. Basic, low-cost versions of these tools are available at local improvement stores if you are a DIY person.

Does insurance cover water damage caused by sewer overflows or water pressure from below ground?

Often, residential insurance policies do not cover sewer backups unless specific sewer backup coverage is added to the policy. Sewer backup coverage is available from most insurers for a nominal cost. You can find out from your insurance agent or spend some time reviewing your insurance policy.

What are the causes of sewer backups?

- **Blockages due to tree roots:** Shrubs and trees seeking moisture can make their way into sewer line cracks, causing extensive damage. This process may start out slowly, but as the tree or shrub continues to grow, so does the root. Tree roots can enter the service pipe at joints and cause blockages. Roots from different types of trees act differently, with some having the potential to travel long distances. If you suspect that city trees are responsible for sewer line damage, your plumber can contact the city and samples of the roots will be used to help identify the trees and who is responsible for cleanup. Sometimes, a blockage is the result of a combination of city and private trees. In this case, the costs are split between the city and the property owner.
- **Sanitary main:** A blockage can occur in a city sanitary main. If the blockage is not detected in time, sewage from the main can back up into homes through floor drains. Usually, this happens slowly, giving the owner time to call a licensed plumber to assess the damage. If water is entering your property at a rapid rate, call the city public works office and report the problem immediately so a city operator can investigate the situation.

- **Water in a basement:** Most basement flooding is not related to the sanitary sewer system. In many cases, soil settles adjacent to the building and, if not removed, leads to rainwater flowing towards the building and down the outside of the foundation wall. This is particularly true in older buildings where cracks may have developed in the foundation or floor slab, allowing water to enter the basement. The cement floor and basement walls of these structures may have deteriorated to the point that they are no longer waterproof. Thus, water can show up in a basement which has never had a water problem previously. This frequently happens when the ground is saturated after repeated or heavy rainstorms. Drainage can be improved by making sure that water is directed away from a building. Homeowners can also prevent flooding by water-sealing their basements.

Checklist to prevent sewer backups

- **Dispose of grease properly:** Cooking oil should be poured into a heat-resistant container and disposed of only after it cools off. Do not dispose of it in your sink drain. Washing grease down the drain with hot water can cause significant problems. As the grease cools off, it will solidify either in the drain, the property owner's line or in the main sewer, causing the line to constrict and eventually clog.

- **Dispose of paper products properly**: Paper towels, disposable and cloth diapers, and feminine products can cause many problems in a property owner's lateral, as well as in the city main, because they do not deteriorate quickly as bathroom tissue does.

- **Replace your line with a new plastic pipe:** One way to prevent tree roots from entering your line is to replace your line and tape with new plastic pipe. If you still have problems with tree roots growing in your lateral, you may have to have roots cut periodically.

- **Illegal plumbing connections:** Do not connect French drains, sump pumps and other flood control systems to your sanitary sewer. It is illegal, and debris and silt will clog your line. Consult a plumber to correct any illegal connections.

- **Install a backwater prevention valve:** A backwater valve is a fixture installed into a sewer line or drain line in the basement of your property to prevent sewer backflows. A properly installed and maintained backwater valve allows sewage to go out, but prevents it from coming back in. Property owners are responsible for the installation and maintenance of backwater valves. The cost to install one depends on the type of plumbing in your home and the difficulty of installation. Check with a qualified plumber.

A sewer backup can lead to serious illness, destruction of your valuables, damage to your property and can even result in electrical malfunctions. Immediate cleanup of the affected property can help minimize the inconvenience resulting from a backup and can prevent mold and further damage. In the event of sewer backup, promptly arrange for water damage restoration cleanup of your property by a qualified IICRC restoration firm.

What is the water damage restoration process for a sewage backup?

Upon arrival to your property, a trained IICRC certified project manager will begin the assessment of damage and plan for the mitigation of the sewage backup on the property.

Some of the sewage backup assessments we perform include:

- Determining the location of the sewer backup.
- Determining the water's path through the property using thermal imaging equipment.
- Determining areas in the property affected by the sewer backup, including ceilings, walls, flooring, fixtures, mechanical damage, furniture, drapes and personal content.
- Determining the plan of attack. Upon review of the property, the technician will figure out how to remediate the sewer backup, dry your property and what equipment will be used.

D.I.Y. – Can I handle cleaning up the sewer backup myself?

It is not advised to clean sewage backups yourself. Water contaminated with sewage usually contains a variety of bacteria, viruses and germs that are harmful to your health. You can experience vomiting, diarrhea, skin rashes or even contract Hepatitis A if you consume contaminated water or food. You can also get sick if you use items that have been in contact with the sewage without disinfecting them properly first (the viruses are not transmitted through the air. Instead, the contaminated pieces can easily get in touch with consumables, kitchen utensils, medicines, toiletries, etc.). Keep in mind that touching such articles with bare hands can cause skin irritation or infection, especially if you have cuts or sores. Professional restoration companies have IICRC trained technicians, appropriate equipment, and the experience necessary for a quick and efficient intervention. A professional restoration company can immediately come up with the most appropriate, safe and least expensive solution, especially if you want your home up and running as quickly as possible. It's not worth risking the health of your family by dealing with this on your own!

What are the three basic categories of water found in water damages?

Category 1: Known as "clean water," this type of water originates from a sanitary source and poses no substantial risk from dermal exposure, ingestion or inhalation. However, it may not always remain clean after it comes into contact with other surfaces or materials. Some examples of "clean water" are broken water supply lines, tub or sink overflows, or appliance malfunctions that involve water supply lines.

Category 2: Known as "grey water," this type of water contains significant contamination and has the potential to cause discomfort or sickness if contacted or consumed by humans. It may contain potentially unsafe levels of microorganisms or nutrients for microorganisms, as well as other organic or inorganic matter (chemical or biological). Examples of this category of water include toilet bowls filled with urine (but not feces), sump pump failures, seepage due to hydrostatic failure and water discharge from dishwashers or washing machines.

Category 3: Known as "black water," this water is grossly contaminated and may contain pathogenic, toxigenic or other harmful agents. Such water sources may carry silt, organic matter, pesticides, heavy metals, regulated materials or toxic organic substances. A sewage backup will typically include category 3 water. Other examples of this type are toilet bowl water (with feces), sewer backup, seawater, rising water from rivers or streams, ground surface water or standing water.

What kind of equipment will be used?

Efficient equipment and technology to get your property sanitized and dry. This advanced technology is necessary to efficiently remove the sewage to efficiently complete the drying and restoration process.

Some of the equipment used for sewage backups include:

- Dehumidifiers
- Air movers
- Negative air fans
- Thermal imaging cameras
- Moisture meters
- Wood floor drying systems
- Desiccants
- Anti-Microbial solutions
- Truck-mounted water extraction units
- Portable water extraction units

How much does a sewer backup clean-up cost?

The average cost of drying out your property, performing restoration services from a "clean" water leak (not gray or black water) can average from **$1,500 - $3,000**. The average cost of drying out your home from black water damage will cost anywhere from **$4,000 and up**. Reconstructing damage done to areas like drywall, baseboards, paneling, carpeting and padding can be anywhere from **$6,000 and up**, depending upon how large the affected area from the water damage is. Restoration costs are based on individual situations and may vary depending upon the conditions.

Who will guide me through the insurance process?

We do!! Your restoration company will help you navigate the insurance process like a much-devoted co-pilot. Review your homeowners' insurance policy to find out if you have sewer backup coverage. Restoration companies follow strict guidelines and use required estimating software administered by insurance companies. This means that you don't have to be the middle person in the process. Your restoration company should work and communicate directly with your insurance provider to ensure your property is properly restored after water damage, bringing your home or property back to its pre-loss conditions.

5. Seven Negative Effects of Water Damage In Your Home

If you experience water damage it can be tempting to believe it's no big deal. Afterall, it is only water, right? Wrong. Gone unchecked, stray H2O can bring about negative effects of water damage in your home. One of the reasons why water damage in your home is so harmful is because water is known as the universal solvent—it dissolves more substances than any other liquid. And in your home, it can dissolve major structural parts and leave behind some really terrible effects of water damage.

Here are seven of the most common negative effects of water damage in your home:

Devalued property

The signs of water damage are difficult to hide. They'll usually reveal themselves to any appraiser even if you attempt to patch affected areas or paint over the stains. Also, when water's left untreated, a repellent smell can linger which will probably turn buyers away.

Structural damage

Structural damage occurs depending on the amount of water surrounding the affected area. Drywall begins to deteriorate and the subfloor can easily warp or even split, meaning you'll end up replacing and restoring the affected areas. Even solid materials that foundations are made of, whether masonry, concrete or stone, can soak up small amounts of water through their cracks and pores. Unless these pockets of water are removed, they can create defects in the building foundation that eventually weaken the entire structure.

Mold

If you've ever owned a home and experienced leaking or flooding, you already know that one of the worst effects of water damage is the growth of mold afterwards. Any presence of water with the right temperature can cause mold to begin growing in as quickly as 48 hours. Once mold is present, it can be very difficult and expensive to <u>treat and remove</u>. Also, if mold is left untreated it can spread and can cause adverse health effects.

Electrical damage

Once electrical systems are damaged by moisture, wiring, outlets and electrical boxes become unsafe to use until they're professionally inspected. Electrical water damage usually occurs to kitchen appliances, washing machines, dryers, hot water tanks, furnaces and low mounted electrical outlets.

Health hazards

A home exposed to flood water is susceptible to harmful bacteria and other microbes. If not treated correctly, toxins will linger on your affected furniture, carpets and inside your HVAC system long after the water has dried. Those bacteria and microbes can cause serious respiratory issues and other health issues.

Damaged personal items

The same water that causes structural damage can quickly destroy many personal items including photographs, books, electronics and personal documents, among other items. However, if you act quickly and call in a water damage expert, you may be able to reverse this negative effect of water damage and save many of your personal items.

And... bugs!

Bugs love moisture and water-damaged areas of your home create the perfect breeding ground for mosquitoes, beetles, fleas, ticks, spiders and more. And, even worse, the hatching eggs and dying bugs will attract even more insects to the area. This is why bacteria is known as one of the worst effects of water damage in your home. As you can see, when water damage occurs in your home, immediate action is needed. That way, you can mitigate the negative effects of water damage and minimize cleaning and restoration costs.

6. How a Disaster May Add Value to Your Property

Property damage from water, fire, mold and storms can feel devastating. While experiencing a disaster, it's hard to find an upside. But a disaster could increase your property value in the long run if you have the right homeowner's coverage and restoration professionals working on the job. For example, when you file a homeowner's claim, your contractor's job is to get the home back to pre-loss condition. But the end result often turns out better, particularly if you live in an older home.

The importance of proper restoration

When you experience damage to your home, it's extremely important to have the loss inspected. Proper restoration is the key to not only maintaining the value of your home, but potentially increasing its value. If damage is left unattended or is incorrectly restored or repaired by DIY efforts or a cut-rate contractor, you run the risk of additional and significant damage in the long run.

Insurance terms to understand

"Pre-loss condition" is an important insurance term and concept. The definition is: the condition property was in the moment before a damage occurred. Assuming your loss is covered under your policy, your insurance will pay to bring your property back to its pre-loss condition with your deductible being your only out of pocket cost.

Besides pre-loss condition, you may also hear the term "comparable materials and quality" when dealing with your insurance company. So, this means that any irreparably damaged materials resulting from the loss will be exchanged with the same or similar material of equal quality. For example, if the laminate flooring in your kitchen gets destroyed, it'll be replaced with laminate flooring of like quality, even if the same flooring no longer exists.

In a home that's relatively new, you probably won't see much of an increase in value. But in an older home, the damage to your property may turn out to be advantageous when decades old flooring, cabinets, carpets, etc., are replaced with brand new furnishings.

When to upgrade

One thing many homeowners aren't aware of is that they can choose to make upgrades in the event of an insurance claim. So, if you were planning a remodel but hadn't saved up for it yet, you may be able to afford it now. This is the time to turn your damage into your benefit. Did you know that your insurance company will still only pay for comparable materials and quality, less your deductible, but they certainly won't complain if you decide to spend extra money out of your pocket to upgrade those materials? In fact, they're happy if you do as they're now insuring a higher quality home and that's a good thing in their book.

What your insurance will cover

As an example of how this would work, let's say your

kitchen cabinets and laminate counter were ruined by water damage. Your insurance will pop for replacement cabinets and a counter of comparable materials and quality, but you've already been thinking about a kitchen remodel and have been saving for a future project. So, you can now combine the money you've been saving and the money the insurance is paying to upgrade to much higher quality materials for a significantly lower out-of-pocket cost. By doing this, you vastly improve your property value, especially when upgrading areas of your home like the kitchen or bathroom that can be expensive to remodel, but are extremely attractive to buyers.*

Whether you upgrade or not, having your home restored professionally should be your highest priority. Doing so not only increases the value of your home, but will also ensure the damage is completely repaired and won't come back to haunt you in the future.

We do not recommend purposely destroying areas of your home you want remodeled so you can save some money! Besides being unethical, your homeowner's policy will not cover intentional acts in which you deliberately try to damage your property.

7. How to Restore Items after They've Been Water Damaged

Hurricanes, heavy rains, flooding, leaky roofs, main water supply leaks, burst pipes... all of these have the ability to cause severe water damage in your home. From destroyed drywall to submerged carpets, water damage can wreak havoc on both a home and the items within it. No matter what the cause of the water damage, nothing is worse than finding your valuables and mementos swimming in a pool of water. Nobody wants to see their prized possessions ruined by water streaking or disintegration. The good news is, homeowners dealing with water damage to valuables are not alone.

Water damage is an everyday part of homeownership. In fact, you can consider yourself lucky if you have yet to experience a water damaged home. It's far more common to deal with one, if not two or three, in a decades' worth of time. That's why you should always make sure your most valuable and sentimental possessions are kept safely out of the way of potential sources of water damage. Having them insured is also a good idea.

In the event of a water damage disaster that does happen to affect valuables, heirlooms and prized possessions, you have options. We receive calls every single day from homeowners whose valuables have been seemingly destroyed by leaks and flooding and we can say honestly that all hope is not lost – no matter how devastated you're feeling at the moment.

The most important thing you can do for your valuables in the immediate aftermath of a water damaging event is to get a good jump on restoring what needs to be restored. The quicker you tend to your possessions, the more likely they will near-fully recover from water damage. Prioritize the items that mean the most to you. How you determine the "meaning" of an item is up to you: By price or by sentimental value are the two we hear most often.

Next, determine what characteristics the water you're dealing with has. Try to take note of if the water is salty, dirty or contaminated, all of which indicate the water is toxic. If your valuables come into contact with toxic water, you'll need to call a professional in because trying to clean the items could pose a health risk. If your valuables were affected by uncontaminated water, you can take immediate steps to restore them before you seek professional help:

Air-dry affected items

Air-drying indoors is the best way to quickly and gently remove water from items. Try to open your windows to increase airflow if the weather permits. If it's hot and humid outside, avoid natural air and instead use fans on low power settings, air conditioners and dehumidifiers to begin drying out items. Do not use hair dryers, irons or exposure to sunlight – all of which can cause further damage.

Clean items gently

Once your possessions are mostly dry, you'll need to start cleaning them of dirt and debris. We recommend using soft microfiber towels and brushes to do this. Remember, even if they were sturdy before, your items are likely hyper-fragile now and should be treated with great care. Photographs should be separated from albums and each other with white paper towels. Same goes for book pages. Avoid rubbing any water damaged item clean, which can cause structural damage and staining.

Pay special attention to photos

Photos and other family documents need immediate attention and should be treated as gently as possible to minimize the risk of ripping and bleeding/streaking. You can clean photos by rinsing them in clean water and then air-drying them on a paper towel.

Buy time

Water damage always seems to happen at the worst, busiest, most frustrating times. With all of the other restoration-related tasks you need to manage, plus maintaining your work and personal life, you might simply not be able to get to restoring every single item you'd like to. Here's a cool trick instead: Freeze photos, papers, books and textiles in the freezer so you can clean them later. Freezing items halts further mold and ink damage and buys you time. Other items that you cannot deal with in the immediate aftermath should be put in open, unsealed boxes or bags.

Dispose of what is ruined

Major storms and floods that cause severe water damage will undoubtedly leave a lot of debris behind – much of which may be unsalvageable. Be selective in what items you choose to focus on restoring and which ones you cut your losses with. Especially those items that are broken or disintegrated. Nobody likes to admit their stuff is ruined but removing the items you can will leave a clutter-free and unobstructed workspace for professional restorers.

Consult a professional

After a water damaging event, you can take the previous steps to initiate the recovery of your items, but you'll likely also need to call in an expert to finish the job. When it comes to restoration, it's better to do too little than to do too much. Leave the heavy lifting to the experts when you are unsure of what steps and procedures to take. Additionally, you'll need to call in a restoration team to repair the water damage done to the structure of your home. The quicker you can get a professional in to clean up the water, inspect for mold and repair damages, the faster your life will return to normal.

8. How Hidden Water Damage Can Affect Your Home

Have you ever witnessed the disappearing water trick, where a magician causes water poured into a cup to magically vanish, as if into thin air? (Spoiler alert: sodium polyacrylate, the stuff in disposable diapers, is first put in the bottom of the cup to soak up the water!)

But water will disappear even without any "magic" involved. It's very adept at hiding and can be exceedingly difficult to find. In fact, it sometimes hides so effectively that it can't be detected unless special meters that sense the presence of water are used. Why is this important to know? Because even though water is essential for life, it's also one of nature's most destructive elements. Water damage is no joke and can seriously affect the structure of your home. Read on to learn how hidden water can damage your home.

Where can you find hidden water in your home?

Water can be elusive because of the way that it moves. It spreads out like the letter "T" – moving out and downward from its source. Even if water looks to be sitting still, it really isn't. Gravity continues to pull it down into the surface of the material it's resting on. As it moves, it spreads and soaks into whatever porous materials it comes into contact with. After spreading out and down, it has another trick up its sleeve: It can also move upward. For example, because of capillary action in porous materials, water sitting at the base of drywall can wick up the wall at a rate of one inch per hour during a 24-hour period!

Because of water's sneaky ways and the multiple causes for its infiltration in your home, you can find it hidden in a variety of places in the home. For example, water hides behind insulation, inside electrical boxes and outlets, behind walls and cabinets, and in subfloors. Even if a surface feels dry, there may still be moisture hiding underneath or inside of it. What this can mean for your home is that secondary damage like mold or warping can occur. It can even ruin expensive hardwood floors. Of course, where water hides it also causes damage in your home. That's why it's important to act fast when you do find it.

What should you do?

Water damage is a serious issue in most older homes. So, when you find water hidden in your home, don't delay! The longer water is left sitting in your home, the more damage it creates. Hesitating to acknowledge the problem also increases the drying time, adding to the costs of remediation.

When you find water hidden in your home, don't DIY the cleanup. Instead, make sure you call in the professionals, or else you'll risk not actually mitigating the water damage. Certified technicians are able to sniff out hidden water in your home with specialized moisture meters and thermal imaging cameras. With this equipment, they are able to locate the confines of the affected area and show you the scope of the damage. Then, any moisture is removed using dehumidifiers and air mover fans to ensure that no further damage occurs, bringing your property back to pre-loss condition.

9. How to Shield Your Home from Moisture and Humidity

It's humid in many cities, but it's during the summer that we really feel it. According to Tom Skilling, chief meteorologist at WGN-TV, in Chicago, for example, the high summer-time humidity has three primary origins: humid air that arrives here from the Gulf of Mexico, moisture that's released by growing plants and moisture that evaporates into the air from wet soil. Surprisingly, the lake actually removes moisture from humid summer air. Just as water vapor condenses out of humid air onto a cold glass of soda, so also does moisture from humid air condense onto the cool surface of Lake Michigan. And when that "dehumidified" air blows across Chicago, our air actually dries out.

No matter the season, protecting your home from moisture and humidity is the key to living comfortably and preventing substantial damage. By maintaining the indoor humidity level of your home between 30 and 50 percent, you can experience significant benefits. Along with enjoying a preferred comfort level, a lower indoor humidity setting prevents excess moisture which has the destructive tendency to rot a home's wood furniture, drywall and window frames. Other household items, such as musical instruments, likewise react adversely to dampness.

Maintaining low humidity also reduces the chances of mold getting a foothold and uncontrollably spreading throughout your home. Additionally, dust mites, some allergens and pest infestations have less of a chance to thrive in a properly humidified environment.

Steps to take to reduce humidity

Each home handles humidity differently. Factors that influence how a house responds to humidity include the home's construction and design, the airtightness of the home and if the builder installed vapor barriers.

The following are some ways you can help reduce moisture and high humidity levels to protect your home:

- **Insulate crawl spaces**—Crawl spaces are notorious for containing excess moisture and high humidity levels. These damp environments are a breeding ground for mold colonies. Rotted joists and damage to the home's structure can result. Before installing insulation in crawl spaces, any standing water will need to be removed and the ground dried before laying down a vapor barrier.

- **Insulate the basement**–Many basements have problems with condensation which forms when moist air hits cold pipes, walls and exposed duct work. Adding insulation to these problem areas prevents the humid air from reacting to cooler surfaces.

- **Run the air conditioner**–Did you know that air conditioning units help to dehumidify because the refrigeration process naturally gets rid of some of the moisture in the air? That's why you see them dripping when running. If you don't have an AC unit, then run a fan. It won't directly remove moisture, but a few hours a day of steady air flow will help lessen minor dampness.

- **Run a dehumidifier**–Installing a dehumidifier will efficiently reduce humidity in high-moisture spaces like the basement. Mold grows in environments with humidity levels above 60 percent, so it should be set significantly lower than that. Monitor the dehumidifier; if the unit never shuts off, it is a sign of an air leak.

Possible underlying problems

Possible factors contributing to moisture and high humidity in your home may be:

- A leak in your plumbing system
- Water entering your home due to clogged gutters
- Cracked sealants around windows and drains
- Landscaping or pavement sloping toward the house

10. What to Do If I've Got a Faulty Waterline?

We've compiled this checklist of things that you can do to help stabilize your property after the discovery of a faulty water supply line.

Why should I care about my waterline?

The main waterline is the primary pipe that brings water into the property. This pipe is typically located underground and connects your property to your community's water source. Your waterline is not the same as your private sewer lateral, which removes used water and sewage from your property. Since water lines remain underground and under constant pressure, it is easy for them to break and cause water to flow to surface levels. Though this may seem like something fairly easy to deal with, faulty water lines can lead to contaminated water entering your property, presenting significant health hazards to those in the building.

What steps should I take if my waterline is faulty?

When you discover or even suspect that your waterline is faulty, you should do the following:

- Shut off all appliances and avoid drinking or using tap water. There should almost always be a shutoff valve somewhere on the property that will allow you to cut off the flow of water through the primary pipe in the event of an emergency.

- Turn off the water. Sometimes your public utility service will shut off the water before you even notice there is a problem, but if this does not occur you can always find the property-owner shutoff valve and turn off the water yourself. You will need a water meter key to do this.
- Call a plumber. After you manage to get the water to stop flowing, be sure to call a plumber ASAP so they can fix the problem before the water starts to damage your property beyond repair.

What is the water damage restoration process for a faulty waterline?

Upon arrival at your property, a trained IICRC certified project manager will begin the assessment of any damage and will plan the mitigation of the water's damage to the property. Some of the faulty waterline assessments performed include:

- Identifying the specific location of the waterline and the subsequent water damage to your property.
- Determining the water's path throughout the property using thermal imaging equipment.
- Determining areas in the property affected by the water damage, such as ceilings, walls, flooring, fixtures and mechanical damage.
- Determining the best plan of attack. We will determine the best way to dry your property and what equipment we'll use to do it.

D.I.Y. – Can I handle cleaning up any water damage or faulty waterlines myself?

Simple drying techniques are often not enough when drying water in the aftermath of a leak, spill or flood. Carpets, walls, paneling, baseboards and floor coverings are porous, which means extensive water damage cleaning is required. Surface cleaning only removes visible contamination, but microorganisms are often left behind, which can potentially cause health problems, unpleasant odors or, worst of all, mold growth. All surfaces affected by water damage must be thoroughly cleaned, dried, disinfected and deodorized by a trained professional in order to properly eliminate disease-causing bacteria, fungi and viruses.

11.The Three Warning Signs Indicating a Broken Pipe

Many times a plumbing problem is noticeable, like when it's raining from the ceiling or a small river begins flowing from under your bathroom door. Sometimes broken or damaged pipes aren't that obvious in your home, but they may still let you know there's a problem if you pay attention to the warning signs. By doing so, you can tackle the problem in its infancy and avoid the destruction and pricey repairs that are sometimes associated with water damage. So, here are three signs to watch out for:

Strange sounds

Do you ever notice a whistling sound in your home?

You're not doing it, no one else in the house is doing it and unfamiliar dogs are showing up at your door? Well, whistling or whining also happens when plumbing gets dented. The sound starts when water is no longer capable of flowing freely through a pipe. This problem intensifies water pressure and can eventually cause a pipe to burst.

Those sounds may also be the sign of a broken-down pressure-reducing valve. Without being replaced, it could cause burst pipes, overflows and other problems over time.

Putrid smells

Another sign of a broken pipe are odd or horrible odors. A common origin of these smells emanates from a p-trap. The p-trap is the U-shaped pipe under your sink or toilet that retains a small amount of water that acts as a preventative seal that keeps sewer gasses from discharging into your home. If a break causes that water to seep out of the p-trap, then you will smell the odor of sewage.

Likewise, when pipes get broken or clogged, sewage can't flow through the plumbing system properly. It's vital that you deal with these problems promptly as sewage can pose a considerable health risk to your family and pets.

Uncommon sights

Are you blaming puddles in your home on your pets or kids? That may be one answer, but if they continually appear, particularly in the same area, then that could be a sign of broken or damaged plumbing.

Another strange (and frightening) sight that may indicate

a broken pipe is an unusually high water bill. Elevated usage could be triggered by leaky toilets, faucets or plumbing. Or the problem may be that an underground pipe feeding water from your meter to your home has developed a crack or loose joint. This issue can be produced by aged pipes, seismic activity, tree roots or animal actions.

Broken pipes aren't unusual and can typically be quickly and easily fixed by a professional, but don't put it off. The longer you do, the more damage will be created and the more expensive it'll be to repair.

12. Why Pipes Freeze and How to Stop It From Happening to You

About the only time you want to hear the sounds of snap, crackle and pop is from a fireplace or your breakfast cereal, but never from the water pipes in your property. Once one ruptures, it can release hundreds of gallons per hour, causing extensive water damage to your property. Unfortunately, we see this happen all the time during long winters when pipes are allowed to freeze, but why do they break?

Water's weird quality

Water reacts very differently from most other elements. When water cools, it contracts until it reaches approximately 40°F. After that, it expands slightly until it reaches the freezing point, when it then swells by about 9%. Since that's enough pressure to split open boulders, your pipes don't stand a chance!

Recognize the problem areas

The pipes that are more likely to freeze are:

- Those exposed to severe cold, like outdoor hose spigots, swimming pool supply lines and water sprinkler lines.
- Water pipes in unheated interior areas like basements, crawl spaces, attics, garages or kitchen cabinets, especially those that aren't insulated.
- Pipes that run along outside walls that have little or no insulation.

Nip it in the bud

Here are steps you can take before and after cold weather sets in to help keep your pipes from freezing and bursting:

- Drain water from your swimming pool and water sprinkler supply lines.
- Close inside valves that supply outdoor spigots, then open the spigots to let any remaining water drain out. Keep outside valves open so that any water left in the pipe can expand without breaking it.
- Add high R-value insulation to attics, basements and crawl spaces.
- Install "pipe sleeves" or wrap UL-listed "heat tape," "heat cable" or similar materials onto exposed water pipes.
- Keep garage doors closed if there's a water supply line inside.

- Open kitchen and bathroom cabinets to let warmer air circulate around the plumbing.
- Once the temperature reaches 28°F outside, let water drip from both the cold and hot water faucets. This not only keeps water moving through the pipes, but relieves built-up water pressure should they freeze.
- Keep the thermostat set to the same temperature day and night. A slightly higher electric bill costs less than a repair job on a broken pipe and subsequent water damage.
- If you're a snowbird and will be gone for a while, leave the heat in your home set to no lower than 55°F.

Many times, a frozen pipe will burst in the middle of the night when it's coldest. Unfortunately, that's also the time you're usually asleep, so you may not be aware of the problem until hours later, compounding the water damage and the cost to repair it. So, do all you can to ensure that it doesn't happen to you.

13. What to Do About Frozen and Burst Pipes

Often in cold weather regions, plunging sub-zero temperatures and rapid warm-ups can cause pipe bursts. Water damage in residences, as well as office buildings, churches, schools and multi-family residential buildings, caused by burst pipes is an enormous inconvenience and hazard to homeowners, landlords, and property managers alike. When temperatures drop well below zero, property owners are faced with significant threats to property safety from frozen and burst pipes. When temperatures fall below zero degrees, pipes are incredibly vulnerable and cause major home damage. Since they can quickly turn into a very expensive problem for homeowners, we want to make certain you are aware how to prevent pipes from freezing, how to thaw pipes if they do freeze, and what to do if frozen pipes end up bursting and causing vast water damage to your property.

Why do pipes burst in cold weather?

Cold weather can result in serious issues if your pipes are affected in your home. Although cold temperatures generally cause things to contract, ice has more volume than water. This means that when water freezes inside a pipe, it expands and increases in pressure. The building pressure must escape, causing the pipe to eventually burst. This can sometimes occur at a weak joint in the pipe, but pressure can also burst right out of the side of the pipe wall as well. One way to prevent water pipes from bursting during extreme cold is to turn on your faucets occasionally to allow a slow but steady stream of water to escape. Be sure to not let out too much water, you only need to release a trickle for this trick to work. When done correctly, this tactic will keep water moving through your pipes and prevent pressure from building up inside them.

How to prevent pipes from freezing

While you might think that homes in cold weather regions would be built to withstand the cold, many do a poor job surviving the winter without significant damage. Within homes, there are areas where pipes are more likely to incur damage due to freezing temperatures. Some of these places include:

- Outdoor areas (hose bibs, waterlines to irrigation systems, wells or pools)
- Unheated areas (garage, attic, crawl space or basement)
- Cabinets, where pipes cannot get enough heat when cabinet doors are closed (under the kitchen or bathroom sink)
- Uninsulated exterior walls

Once you've determined what pipes may be susceptible to freezing, you will want to take action to protect those pipes when temperatures plummet:

- Open cabinets. This allows the warm air to circulate around pipes.
- If there are pipes in the attic, open the door to allow warm air to move upwards.
- Let water trickle from faucets. The constantly flowing water will prevent pipes from freezing. The small amount of water you waste is much less than the cost of a plumbing repair or the amount of water that will escape if a pipe bursts.

These tips may get you through a handful of cold nights, but in general, we recommend preemptively insulating pipes during your home winterizing process.

How to insulate pipes

Insulating pipes is by far the best way to prevent pipes from freezing. After you've identified what pipes need insulation, visit the hardware store and pick up your insulating material of choice. You can use:

- Tubular sleeve insulation
- Fiberglass insulation
- Duct tape
- Foil insulation tape
- Heating blanket tape
- In a pinch, use newspaper and duct tape

Prepare the pipes. A simple wipe down with soapy water will do the trick. Wrap the pipes with the material you've chosen. Be sure to cover all exposed surfaces. Secure the edges and corners with duct tape. If you use fiberglass insulation, wrap the insulation with sheets of plastic or duct tape as well.

Other ways to prevent pipe freezing

If you have pipes in your crawl space, you may want to:

- Insulate the outer walls of your crawl space with foam board

- Close the vents (just during the freeze; crawl spaces need to breathe)
- Run a very low-temp space heater on the lowest setting in the crawl space (away from all flammable materials)

If you have a well, you can:

- Insulate the exposed pipes
- Install a low-watt heat lamp designed for this purpose
- Cover the well to keep heat inside and cold out (look for fiberglass rocks or well covers at the hardware store)

If you have an irrigation system or pool/pond lines, you should:

- Drain the lines
- Use the blow-out-method to remove the remaining water from the lines

If you don't have time to insulate pipes, and you want to prevent frozen and burst pipe damage, consider using heat tape, a heat lamp or a low-watt bulb to heat the space where the pipes are located, but be mindful of fire hazards and install with care. Never use a blow torch or a heat gun when thawing pipes, and exercise care when using a heat lamp.

How to tell if your pipes are frozen
Sometimes you won't be able to protect your pipes until

it is too late, and other times pipes will freeze even despite your best efforts. If you suspect your pipes are frozen, you'll need to take action right away. Here are four major tip-offs:

- You don't have any running water, or you turn on the water and only a trickle comes out of the faucet
- You notice frost or condensation on your pipes
- Pipes feel frozen to the touch
- The pipe is visibly cracked or split in a place you never noticed before

Once you've confirmed a pipe is frozen, you'll need to figure out where the frozen section is located. Oftentimes, an entire pipe won't freeze – instead, just a section of a pipe will freeze ranging from a few inches to one foot. Since pipes with greater exposure are more likely to freeze, first check under the sinks, in the crawl space or basement, in the attic, along the main pipeline to and from your yard, and any other exterior pipes.

If one faucet is fine and another in a different room on the same floor isn't, the pipe is frozen somewhere between the mainline and that room's piping. If the faucets work on one floor but not another, the frozen pipe is located where the floors separate. If no faucets work, a section of the pipe near the main waterline may be frozen.

Can't find the cold section of pipe? It's probably hidden in the wall or yard. Outdoor water lines can be trickier to catch because you probably don't use the pipes leading to a pool or hot tub, irrigation systems or outdoor hoses during the winter. Inspect outdoor lines once in a while if temps stay low.

How to thaw frozen pipes

Once you've found the section that's frozen, you'll need to carefully thaw the pipe without causing it to burst. Try the following:

- Aim a hair dryer on low or medium (not high) heat at the section of pipe
- Run a space heater on low—but be careful not to place it too close to the pipe (this may take some time, so be patient)
- Wrap the pipe with towels dipped in warm water (you'll need to replace them periodically)
- Wrap the pipe with a heating pad on low or medium (not high)

Every once in a while, try running the faucet to see if you've been successful. When water is flowing once again, take steps (see above) to prevent the pipe from freezing again.

How to tell if a frozen pipe has cracked

The danger of frozen pipes is cracking and bursting. Water expands when frozen, and pipes may crack under the pressure of the expansion.

Other signs of a leak include:

- A heavy flow of water, puddles on the floor and/or obvious water damage in the home
- The sound of rushing water inside your wall or floor
- Hot or cold spots inside the wall or floor
- Water stains on the wall or ceiling

Unfortunately, a lot of cracked pipes happen in hidden places where you can't see evidence of the leak. After thawing your pipes, you will want to keep an eye on your water bill. If you see a water bill spike, there's a very good chance you've got a hidden leak. A restoration professional will use leak detection equipment to locate the leak.

14. How to Winterize Your Home

When the leaves are changing colors and summer cookouts have turned into afternoons of apple picking, this also means that lower temperatures and inclement weather are on their way. As hard as it can be to face, it's time to start preparing for the winter and winterize your home.

When it comes to emergency preparedness, residential property owners should prioritize staying one step ahead of inclement weather by ensuring their homes are ready for winter as soon as possible. While it might not feel "cold enough" yet (something we hear all the time from customers!), it's important to complete repairs and winterization measures that will increase the comfort of your family before the weather gets too cold, windy and snowy to get them done. Plus, winterizing your home now could save you money on your heating bills when the temperatures become frigid.

We understand that homeowners may want to winterize their home, but find it confusing. It's a topic we often get questions about, usually in the form of, "What should I do to winterize my home?" As professionals, we have seen it all and when it comes to winterizing, we understand what works, what doesn't work, the must-do's and the nice-to-do's.

Here are our top 10 hacks to winterizing your home to increase comfort and save more money:

- **Close up your fireplace:** Before snow accumulates on the roof, check to see that your fireplace flue fully closes. You shouldn't be able to feel any cool air blowing in when the flue is closed. If it can't fully close, make sure you complete necessary repairs before the winter—or try installing glass doors around your fireplace to keep unwanted cold air out.
- **Replace weatherstripping around doors:** Weatherstripping is worn down every year by inclement weather. Check that you cannot see any light coming in at the bottom, sides or top of doors that lead outside. If you can see light, you need to replace the weatherstripping—which is quite easy and affordable compared to the cost of your heating bill if hot air is escaping around your doors.
- **Invest in heavier drapes and rugs:** Replacing light summer drapes and rugs for heavier alternatives is a good way to increase the insulation on your floors and windows. Opting for something heavier will keep the heat in a contained space better, negating the need for a blasting heater all the time.
- **Get an energy audit:** Many utilities companies will provide customers with free basic energy audits to identify where hot air is leaking from their home.

They can also suggest improvements that will increase energy efficiency in the colder months.

- **Identify areas where insulation can be improved:** Check your attic and crawl spaces for insulation deterioration (this is normal, natural and common). Make sure you add more insulation material before the cold hits if you notice any deterioration to properly winterize your home.

- **Install a programmable thermostat:** Save money on your heating bill by investing in a newer, programmable thermostat that can automatically set the temperature lower when your family is not home.

- **Lower your water heater temperature:** You can save money on hot water by lowering the water heater baseline temperature with little effect on your hot water supply. Most water heaters are set much higher than the recommended 120 degrees Fahrenheit. Check to see if yours is and if so, drop the temperature settings to 120 degrees and save money and energy with no negative impacts on your hot water.

- **Cover your water heater:** You may be losing money on the heat escaping from your hot water tank. Try buying a water heating blanket from your local hardware store and covering the tank with it to keep the heat in.

- **Change furnace filters:** When your filters are dirty, your furnace has to work harder. Experts recommend that homeowners change their filters monthly when the furnace is in use.

- **Add caulking around windows:** If the area around your windows has cracks, cold air can easily enter the home, while warm air can easily escape. Take some time this fall to check for cracks, and patch or replace the caulking if necessary.

As always, if you have any questions or concerns about completing any of the above guidelines, our professionals are standing by to help. We know it's not necessarily fun to think about the arrival of inclement weather, but a little bit of diligent preparation now can save you time, energy and stress later on. By following our top ten actionable recommendations to winterize your home, you'll increase your family's comfort and save money on your heating bills during wintertime.

15. How to Avoid Water Damage From Your Water Heater

Although most homeowners rarely think about it, the fact remains: your water heater will eventually fail. When it does, you may experience catastrophic water damage. The average tank-style water heater has a typical lifespan of about eight to twelve years. Like any appliance, wear and tear and the inevitable effects of time break down the connections, or even the tank itself, until something gives. So, you might want to imagine your water heater as a ticking time bomb as it nears the 10-year mark.

Keep a lookout for these typical signs of a failing water heater:

- Leaking around the base or on top of the unit
- Your tap water becoming discolored or rusty water looking (indicating corrosion)
- A decrease in your hot water temperature

The most disastrous water heater failure is a complete rupture resulting in the release of hundreds of gallons of water onto your property because the water supply to burst tanks continues to flow. This is usually due to corrosion within the tank or if too much pressure builds up inside your water heater. The long-term stress of contracting and expanding with constant temperature variations can also lead to a sudden rupture of the tank, without warning.

This situation is even more devastating when water heaters are situated within the interior of your home, like in a hallway closet or finished basement. One average-sized water heater tank rupturing in the middle of the night can flood your whole home with an inch or two of water.

Steps to prevent water damage from your water heater

1. The first and best action to take is to regularly inspect and monitor your water heater. Periodically check for moisture around the plumbing connections and pooling water on the top of the tank and in the catch pan that it sits in.
2. If you do notice any water leaks, don't hesitate to call your local plumber or HVAC technician to come out and inspect the unit before the damage gets

worse. Rapid response is the key to avoiding long-term and expensive water or mold damage.

3. If you're renovating your house, relocate the water heater to the garage where the potential for damage is lessened. Also, check your local plumbing codes whether a specially designed metal stand is required for your water heater.

4. Consider purchasing a tankless system that doesn't use a storage tank like typical water heaters. Instead, they produce hot water on demand.

16. How to Avoid Water Damage While on Vacation

We can all use some time *away* from our house and take a vacation. While these are usually fun, happy, relaxing and battery charging events— all that good could come crashing down the minute you get back home if when you open the door you step into standing water. Discovering water damage in your home is a nightmare you'll never want to experience.

To avoid this type of scenario, homeowners must be aware of and put into place the following safeguards to prevent flooding emergencies and water damage while they're away. The preparation and extra leg work can pay off in the form of thousands of dollars saved and peace of mind.

Four steps to take before leaving home

1. **Shut off the main water valve** – Before heading out of town, shut off the main waterline to prevent any chance of water damage while you're away. Many water meter setups have two valves, one on the street side of the meter and one on the house side. In colder climates, you'll typically find the main shutoff in the basement near the front of the house. In warmer climates, it'll be outside your home attached to an exterior wall or in an underground box with a removable lid.

2. **Shut off water supply valves** – If you're unable to shut off the main water supply because you have an automatic sprinkler system or someone is watering the plants while you're gone, shut off the valves to the most common sources of water damage such as dishwashers, ice makers and washing machines, in case a hose cracks. Typical supply stops have a small round or oval handle that you turn clockwise to shut off the flow of water.

3. **Replace water supply lines** – To avoid water damage, especially when you're away from home, be sure to install stainless steel braided water supply lines on your appliances, faucets and toilets. They'll last longer than rubber or plastic hoses and are less likely to leak. They also prevent mice from gnawing through the lines. A pair of washing machine hoses costs less than $20 at home centers. Shorter versions for faucets or a toilet are also available.

4. **Check your gutters** – A 1,000 sq. ft. roof will shed about 620 gallons of water during a 1 inch rainfall. That's a lot of water dumped right next to your basement. So, before leaving on a vacation, check your gutters. Make sure leaves, sticks or other debris aren't blocking the inlet of the downspout and preventing water from flowing down the spout. Also make certain your downspout extensions are discharging the water far from the foundation.

Water damage is more than a nuisance

There are many reasons to take the previous precautions before going on vacation. Besides the headaches and expenses, you may also experience these other problems caused by water damage:

- Structural damage
- Mold
- Health problems
- Bad smells
- Stains
- Electrical damage

17. What Can Happen If You Ignore Water Damage in Your Home

If your property experiences some water damage, but it's small, then it's no big deal, right? Wrong. Even though it's only a little bit of water, ignoring water damage in your home can lead to massive structural damage in the long run.

If you're thinking about ignoring water damage that seems minor, keep in mind water is known as the universal solvent for a good reason–it dissolves more substances than any other liquid. That includes major structural parts of your home. And that's just the tip of the iceberg.

In other words, ignoring water damage could leave your home vulnerable to structure integrity breakdowns that cost far more money to fix than simple water cleanup. Not yet convinced?

Here are seven of the most common negative effects of water damage in your home:

Devalued property

The signs of water damage are difficult to hide. They'll usually reveal themselves to any appraiser even if you attempt to patch affected areas or paint over the stains. Also, when water's left untreated, a repellent smell can linger which will probably turn buyers away.

Structural damage

Structural damage occurs depending on the amount

of water surrounding the affected area. Drywall begins to deteriorate and the subfloor can easily warp or even split, meaning you'll end up replacing and restoring the affected areas. Even solid materials that foundations are made of, whether masonry, concrete or stone, can soak up small amounts of water through their cracks and pores. Unless these pockets of water are removed, they can create defects in the building foundation that eventually weaken the entire structure.

Mold

If you've ever owned a home and experienced leaking or flooding, you already know that one of the worst effects of water damage is the growth of mold afterwards. Any presence of water with the right temperature can cause mold to begin growing in as quickly as 48 hours. Once mold is present, it can be very difficult and expensive to treat and remove. Also, if mold is left untreated it can spread and can cause adverse health effects.

Electrical damage

Once electrical systems are damaged by moisture, wiring, outlets and electrical boxes become unsafe to use until they're professionally inspected. Electrical water damage usually occurs to kitchen appliances, washing machines, dryers, hot water tanks, furnaces and low mounted electrical outlets.

Health hazards

A home exposed to flood water is susceptible to harmful bacteria and other microbes. If not treated correctly, toxins will linger on your affected furniture, carpets and inside your HVAC system long after the water has dried. Those bacteria and microbes can cause serious respiratory issues and other health issues.

Damaged personal items

The same water that causes structural damage can quickly destroy many personal items including photographs, books, electronics and personal documents, among other items. However, if you act quickly and call in a water damage expert, you may be able to reverse this negative effect of water damage and save many of your personal items.

And... bugs!

Bugs love moisture and water-damaged areas of your home create the perfect breeding ground for mosquitoes, beetles, fleas, ticks, spiders and more. And, even worse, the hatching eggs and dying bugs will attract even more insects to the area. This is why bacteria is known as one of the worst effects of water damage in your home.

As you can see, when water damage occurs in your home, immediate action is needed. That way, you can mitigate the negative effects of water damage and minimize cleaning and restoration costs.

18. Three Reasons Why Your Roof Is Leaking

We've all been there: Looked up at the ceiling and noticed damp spots or streaks. Or, even worse, looked up to find water dripping down from these areas. The disheartening telltale signs that the roof is leaking.

For most homeowners, roof leaks are completely unavoidable. They're also frustrating and annoying inconveniences – especially for homeowners going through their first roof leak, or a roof leak that causes lots of water damage within the home. We can't even begin to pinpoint how many frantic calls we get: *"My roof is leaking... **help!"***

After a roof leak, the most important thing you can do is call a restoration company, get the water damage checked out and taken care of and fix your roof. But for many homeowners, this isn't enough. They also need to understand why their roof leaked in the first place.

While roof leaks are common narratives and will happen to almost every home at one point or another, they can be caused by a variety of different things. We like to make sure homeowners who experience a roof leak understand the possible root causes of such a leak. Ultimately, having a good grasp on the problem will identify your roof's risks and help you take steps to prevent further leaks.

If your roof is leaking, one of these three culprits may be the reason:

Old roof

Sometimes, the roof is just plain old. We especially see

this in old-style period homes. Roofs simply don't last forever and it can be hard for homeowners to keep this in perspective when they buy an old home, often forgetting to inquire about the roof in the process!

If the building materials that comprise your roof age past their functional life expectancy, they'll start to break down. You can usually see this in a quick inspection of the shingles and foundation of the roof. It's fairly easy to tell when they have reached their breaking point.

Since any functional issue that compromises the integrity of your roof leaves you at risk for leaking and collapsing, you'll want to make sure you get the building materials replaced and updated on schedule before disaster strikes, if possible.

Poor room ventilation

Remember, your ceiling and your roof are connected and one can either protect or damage the other. In rooms where high moisture is generated due to life activities, condensation can build up on the ceiling and cause serious damage to the roof over time. This includes bathrooms, kitchens, sunrooms, etc. Basically, any room where water is boiled, steam is created, water sits in the open or moisture from the outdoors has free entry.

To fix this issue, make sure these high-risk rooms are properly ventilated at all times.

Punctured roof or obstructed water flow

Some bad news for homeowners: Your roof is, unfortunately, not impervious to damages caused by falling objects and inclement weather. This is one of the most common reasons for roof damage we see and it's one that often goes unrecognized until it's too late.

Hail, falling trees, branches, satellite dishes, animals— you name it—can cause major damage to a roof. That's why most experts recommend that you schedule a roof inspection as soon as possible after heavy storms if you notice even the smallest sign of a leak. This makes sense if your roof was punctured by a falling item, it leaves it open for water to seep into your home and cause costly damage.

Even if your roof was not punctured by a falling object, it can still be affected by debris that sits on it and causes water flow obstructions. If debris blocks water from flowing down your roof in its natural direction, it will likely cause water to pool on your roof. Eventually, that water will wear through the roof, seep into the home, and cause leaks and extensive water damage.

Roof leaks are never fun to deal with, but it's important to understand that they do happen. It's a normal part of life for many homeowners. In the event that you do have a leak, stay calm. You are not alone. First, try to understand the root cause of the roof leak and make sure you can describe it in detail. You'll want to make sure you schedule a roof inspection and repair.

19. What Should I Do If My Wood Floors Are Wet? - An Ultimate Guide

My hardwood floors are water damaged! What should I do?

An unwelcomed event like water or flood damage to your wood floors is overwhelming, frustrating and can be very costly. The destruction that water damage causes to the construction material used in building your property is immediate and, if not mitigated quickly, can be permanent. We provide emergency drying and restoration services to prevent the further destruction of your attractive wooden floors. In many cases, as long as we are called in quickly, we can save your hardwood floors after water damage strikes with our wood floor drying system process. It is important to take note of the multiple causes of water and moisture damage to hardwood floors.

The top five types of hardwood floor moisture issues:
Cupping

When hardwood floors are affected by water damage or too much moisture, a process called cupping begins. This is when the sides of hardwood flooring swell and rise higher than the center of the boards, creating an uneven surface. Typically, eliminating the source of the water damage and drying the floor can save the wood.

Crowning

Crowning is the opposite of cupping. The middle of the board is higher than the board's edges. This can occur when the surface of the floor encounters moisture. It most often occurs when a floor has been sanded too soon after cupping. When this happens, the top edges of the board are sanded off and are therefore lower than the rest of the board when returning to a normal moisture content.

Buckling

Buckling is one of the most extreme reactions to moisture that can occur with hardwood flooring. It happens when the floor expands beyond expansion gaps and literally pulls away from the subfloor, as high as several inches. It's like walking on a raised floor. Once the humidity drops, the floor may shrink back, but you may see spaces between the wood boards.

Splits and cracking

When extensive moisture or humidity causes the wood to expand significantly, adjoining boards start pressing against each other. In extreme cases, this increased pressure can cause the affected boards to lose their structural integrity and crack. The boards themselves may split, check or crack in the center, at the ends or along the grain, damaging the finish. This damage is permanent, because your hardwood floor finish is cracked and the wood is no longer protected.

Gapping

It is normal that when relative humidity is lower than

recommended, wood planks shrink and thin gaps can appear between them. These small gaps between the wood planks are called cracks, gaps or spaces by consumers. Having gaps between your wood planks is normal and a homeowner should be prepared for it to occur. Once humidity levels rise again, the hardwood floor will expand and, normally, most gaps will close up again.

D.I.Y. – Can I handle cleaning up any water damage myself?

If you are a handy, DIY sort of person, there are some steps you can take to dry your hardwood floors. Simple drying techniques are not enough when drying hardwood floors in the aftermath of a leak, spill or flood. Hardwood flooring is porous, which means advanced drying is required because buckling, crowning and problems can appear very quickly after water damage. With hardwood flooring, time is of the essence.

The best DIY tips for drying hardwood floors:

1. Remove wet items from the area. Move any water-soaked content outside in the sun to dry.
2. Use a wet vacuum to soak up as much of the water as possible. Even when you have removed all the visible water, continue suctioning as the vacuum is still removing water from invisible pores in the wood. This may take some time.
3. Clean the surface of the hardwood floor by scrubbing with a non-sudsy disinfectant. Any

leftover dirt or debris could store water in the pores of the floor. Once you're done, use the wet vacuum to, once again, remove any leftover water remnants.

4. Place a dehumidifier in the center of the room and turn it up to full power. Leave it running for at least 24 hours to ensure it has time to pull out any moisture from the floorboards.

5. Use several fans on full blast in the room as well to aid the dehumidifier.

6. Once the floor is dry, check for any visible signs of mold or mildew. If you see any mold or mildew, immediately scrub the floor with a brush using a mixture of baking soda and water and don a face mask or respirator. This is very important, as the effects of breathing mold can be extremely dangerous to you and your family.

7. Use a moisture testing meter to ensure all the moisture has been removed. Remember, completely drying hardwood floors is a process that could take several weeks. Until you are absolutely certain there is no moisture present, leave the dehumidifier running in the room.

What is the water damage drying process for wooden floors?

Upon arrival at your property, our trained IICRC certified project manager will begin the assessment of water damage and develop a plan to save your hardwood flooring.

Some of the assessments we perform include:

- Determining the cause or source of the water damage to your property
- Determining the water's path through the property using thermal imaging equipment
- Determining areas in the property affected by the water damage, i.e. ceilings, walls, flooring, fixtures, mechanical damage, etc.
- Determining the plan of attack, how we will dry your property and what specialized equipment (including wood floor drying mats) we'll use to do it

20. Top Tips for Preventing Basement Seepage

Even though it may not feel like it to a homeowner experiencing water damage in the lower level of their home, leaking basements are common occurrences in homes throughout the country. After all, any type of foundation can spring a leak, especially as the weather continues to worsen throughout the holiday season.

Leaky basements experience something called basement seepage, which is when water finds ways to enter your basement and pool on your floor, causing it to flood and damage your property.

What causes it? Essentially, water or moisture in basements come from two major sources: indoor humidity that condenses on cold surfaces or water that comes from outside. Rainwater, melting snow or groundwater can saturate the soil around your foundation and leak into your home. Water can leak through cracks or it can even penetrate basement walls in the form of water vapor.

How do you fix it? Though several solutions are available to reduce the amount of water that enters your basement, there is no foolproof answer to resolve the problem.

Step one:

The first thing you should do once you notice basement seepage is to check the walls where the water is entering. Try to determine if the water is entering along a single wall entirely underground, along multiple walls or on one side of the house only.

To figure out what's causing the problem, tape aluminum foil to your basement wall and inspect it a few days later. Moisture on the outside surface of the foil indicates high indoor humidity. Moisture behind the foil means moisture is leaking through the walls.

Step two:

Once you determine the source of the water, start looking for cracks in the affected area. Apply an epoxy during the months when the walls remain dry to seal up cracks. Make sure you squeeze the epoxy well into the walls to make sure that a tight bond is created.

Step three:

Start working to remove excess humidity from the area.

This will help you dry out your basement. Seal leaky dryer vents with foil tape to prevent unwanted humid air from entering your basement. After doing this, you can remove any excess water that has started to pool on your floors.

You can also add a vent fan to your basement bathroom and make sure your family turns it on during showers. Keep your basement windows closed during humid weather. And if you're still getting condensation on cool surfaces, you can run a dehumidifier to lower the indoor humidity.

How do you prevent this from happening in the first place? Make sure that any damaged gutters are repaired or replaced to ensure that no more water enters your basement. Gutters are generally the cause of basement seepage since they are prone to drainage issues. You can place cement splash pads along the gutter in order to carry water away from your house foundations.

Another way you can continue to prevent water from entering your basement is by creating a slope away from the outside foundation of your home. Add dirt next to the outside basement wall so that it slopes down two inches for every foot. This will help from water pooling around your home.

You should also apply a layer of waterproofing on the inside of your basement walls. Make sure you spray the waterproofing in an even application. Hold the spray at least 10 inches away from the basement walls and spray from side-to-side until the wall is covered. Spray one wall at a time. Allow it to dry completely for two to three days before spraying another wall to ensure the proper application.

Finally, it's important to note that condensation dripping

from cold pipes can also contribute to basement water problems. Cover cold water pipes with foam pipe insulation to stop condensation.

21. How to Prevent Ice Dams

Here in the Midwest, temperatures are influx all the time. One day, you're ditching your gloves and hat at home because the sun's out and temperatures are on the rise, and the next day you're groaning at the subzero weather as you walk out of your home wearing three layers of coats.

The up-and-down temperatures in the Midwest are more than just aggravating wildcards for your attire choices – they also pose a big threat to your home's safety. Specifically, temperatures that melt the snow one day and turn the left-over liquid into ice the next can cause ice dams to form on your roof.

Ice dams are caused by a combination of poor attic or roof ventilation and a warm attic space. They can also be exacerbated by a clogged or poorly draining gutter system. An ice dam is a ridge of ice that forms at the edge of a roof and prevents melting snow (water) from draining off the roof. The water that backs up behind the dam can leak into a home and cause damage to walls, ceilings, insulation and other areas.

In other words, ice dams are bad news for your home, and they pose structural and sanitary threats if they are ignored. In the best cases, ice dams cause simple water damage to your roof's drywall which could accumulate mold. In the worst cases, ice dams cause gutter damage and roof collapse, along with serious water damage to your home and belongings. If you notice ceiling leaks or hear creaks or pops, you'll want to call a professional right away! Hopefully, ice damming will not be a problem for you and your family as we head into the homestretch of winter.

Here are some of our top tips to help prevent ice dams on your roof and keep disaster at bay:

Increase ventilation

The most effective long-term solutions are to keep heat out of the attic and to promote ventilation under the roof deck to keep it as cold as possible. The underside of the roof deck must be close to the temperature of the exterior side of the roof. In order to increase ventilation, you might want to think about a soffit-and-ridge vent system. It usually requires insulation baffles installed at the lower side of the roof, more above the exterior walls. The baffles hold back the insulation by a couple of inches, creating a channel for air to flow freely past the insulation. Without them, thick insulation can block the air coming in through the soffit vents, eliminating airflow. If you are a home restoration DIY extraordinaire, this can be done as a project over a weekend. If you – like most people! – are not, give us a call to come take a look and see if we can give your insulation system an upgrade.

Minimize heat sources in the attic

Proper ventilation alone will not prevent ice dams if you

have active heat rejection into the attic. Heat from uninsulated or leaky recessed can lights in the room below add heat to the attic from the light source (light bulb) and allow heated air from the living space to escape into the attic. Other potential heat sources in the attic include uninsulated ductwork and improperly vented bathroom exhaust fans.

Increase attic floor insulation

Prevent heat from your living space from warming your attic with proper amounts of insulation in the attic floor. Sealing air leaks in the ceiling is just as—if not more—important than insulation.

Keep gutters clean

Get rid of all those fall leaves before the snow comes. Also make sure your downspouts are functioning properly. Melted snow has nowhere to go if the gutters are clogged.

Install heat tape

Electric heat tape can help in limited situations with light snow. However, heat tape during heavy snow can cause an ice dam to move further up the roof or make it worse, especially if the gutters are not cleared. Proper installation is important: the tape should serpentine along the roof edge and run inside the gutter and down into the downspout.

Stay on top of roof snow removal

If you keep the snow that piles up on your roof to a minimum, you're less likely to have enough moisture on the roof to go through the melt-and-freeze cycle. Invest in an aluminum roof rake with an extendable handle to help you rake the snow off your roof after heavy snowfalls. Removing at least the lower four feet of snow from the roof edge can help you prevent ice dams from forming. You can do this from the ground. Never get on your roof to remove the snow!

PART 2:

FIRE

Overall, fire smoke and soot damages are one of the most difficult mitigation projects in the restoration industry that require imagination, creativity and attention to detail. Cleaning after fire damage requires hyper attention to minutia. In addition to walls, ceilings and floors, attention must be paid to the HVAC system and things you may not think of, such as light bulbs, which can emit smoke odor once lit and heated. Others are: outlets, light switches, clothing, bedding and even the pillow you lay your head to sleep on. These damages also require a special odor killing machine which releases a gas that follows the same path the smoke and soot damage took when initially spreading through the property. While water damages can be contained, smoke and soot damage due to fire cannot. Smoke odor and soot will travel with air movement and can end up in HVAC systems which mechanically force smoke odor and soot to areas not otherwise affected by fire. This is what makes fire smoke and soot clean up so difficult. Fire smoke and soot damage is very intricate and requires painstaking attention to detail in as far as cleaning and mitigation is concerned.

1. Residential Fire Damage 101: What Do I Do If There's a Fire in My Home?

Damaging fires, unfortunately, happen every 24 seconds in the United States, according to the National Fire Protection Association. While the number of fires and fire-related deaths has been trending down since the 1970s, they still continue to wreak havoc all across the country.

Residential properties are no exception to this reality. In fact, an average of 382,397 fires that occur in the United States happen on residential properties. These fires typically result in nearly 12,000 civilian injuries and over $7,298,475,292 in property damage.

Dealing with an emergency like this is extremely stressful and often unplanned for. We are equipped to handle the aftermath of incidents like this in any kind of residential property.

What do I do if there's a fire in my home?

- Act immediately but stay calm.
- Alert everyone in the home and make sure to leave the property immediately. Use your pre-planned escape route if you have one. Consider developing one now if you don't.
- When everyone is evacuating the building, make sure everyone stays low and crawls since smoke rises.

- Do not stop to retrieve any valuables or collectibles.
- Do not stop to find your pets and help them out of the home.
- If you can, close the door to the room the fire started in and close doors as you continue to exit the building.
- Before opening any closed doors on your way out, touch it with the back of your hand. If the door is warm, then there is likely to be fire behind it and you must find an alternative route to exit the building.
- Do not attempt to extinguish a fire unless you are trained to do so.
- Do not go back into the building.
- Call the fire department as soon as you safely have the opportunity to do so. If there is anyone remaining in the building, make sure to inform them of this.

What should I do after the fire department leaves?

Once the fire is extinguished and the dust settles, call a restoration company immediately to address the damage. Only those who are equipped to handle the water, smoke, and fire damage your home has suffered should be entering the building and handling the situation.

What are the steps for a residential fire damage restoration?

Basically, the main two areas of fire damage clean up are structural cleaning and content cleaning for residential properties that have been affected by smoke or fire damage. The following is a brief description of those services.

Structural cleaning services

1. Structural cleaning involves the cleaning of the property itself. This covers soot sponging of walls and ceilings, including crown molding and baseboards.
2. In some cases, using a soft detergent to clean walls and ceilings.
3. Cleaning of floors, doors and windows.
4. Cleaning of all flat surfaces including countertops and windowsills.
5. Cleaning of all ventilation and duct systems for HVAC.

Content cleaning services

6. Cleaning of all soft goods including garments, drapes, bedding, carpet and upholstery.
7. Cleaning of all electronics and appliances.
8. Drying and restoration of documents.
9. Art Restoration.
10. Cleaning of bookshelves, shelving, furnishings and light fixtures.

What equipment is used?

Air scrubbers: Air scrubbers use high-efficiency particulate air (HEPA) filtration to remove particles from the air, enhancing the efficiency for cleaning and clearing the air for safe breathing. Please do not move or turn off this equipment.

Thermal fogging: This process neutralizes odor, using a strong deodorizer that penetrates everywhere the smoke travels and will require the removal of pets, plants and humans occupants for a short period of time.

Ozone: Ozone is an oxidizing agent produced by a portable ozone generator. This process will require the removal of pets, plants, and human occupants for a short period of time.

OdorKlenz technology: This environmentally friendly deodorizing process removes odors and particulates using OdorKlenz air cartridges in traditional air scrubbers. Safe for people, pets and plants.

How much will it cost?

The costs of fire and smoke damage cleaning and restoration depend on the insurance provider you have. Well-known insurance companies, —including State Farm, Allstate, Liberty Mutual, Hanover, Chubb, Asco, Progressive, Travelers, USAA, Farmers, Nationwide, AIC, Zurich, American Family and Erie, among others, —can recommend a list of quality preferred restoration companies in your area. This means that these quality restoration vendors prescribe to the strict guidelines and to the required estimating software administered by insurance companies and provide a direct pipeline to your insurance company.

2. What Is Fire Content Cleaning?

House fires are one of the biggest causes of property loss in America. But while some items are left in ashes after a fire, not all property is completely ruined. Instead, after a house fire, the property is most often partially damaged—oftentimes by smoke. If you are facing the aftermath of a house fire and your belongings have incurred smoke damage, we have you covered with our guide to fire content cleaning.

Smoke damage is one of the worst side effects of a house fire. When a fire occurs and smoke rises from the flames, its microscopic particles are suspended in the air until they settle on surfaces and items around the house. The soot that covers your belongings is what causes the awful smokey smell and black residue that a fire leaves behind. And, while the stain and smell are frustrating, the real concern is that they are toxic and expose house residents to unwanted chemicals.

It's important to work quickly to mitigate the smoke damage and restore your belongings. Any content recovery that involves removing smoke/fire damage from the fibers of an item (clothes, furniture, photos, housewares, etc.) is called fire content cleaning. While some people choose to go the DIY route for cleanup after a fire, we must recommend that you hire a professional restoration company, to ensure that the fire content cleaning process provides your belongings the highest chance of full recovery.

Establish safety

The first concern in every fire damage cleanup situation is safety. An essential part of this safety is understanding the state of indoor air quality. After a fire, indoor air contains floating smoke and soot particles, which are carcinogens and could be both toxic and dangerous. Our team comes equipped with respirators and other safety equipment and clothing to protect against soot exposure. We'll also increase ventilation to help toxic contaminants exit the indoor air naturally. The presence of unsafe air and the need for expert safety measures is why it's so important to call in a professional restoration crew to handle fire content cleaning and fire/smoke damage.

Evaluate the damaged items

Next, it is necessary to determine which items should be cleaned and where, as well as which items are unsalvageable and will need to be discarded. Item material, cost, cost of restoration, antique value and homeowner desires are taken into account when evaluated for repairability. The restoration company will assess affected items quickly to minimize the soot damage that can be incurred in just a few hours or days after the initial fire.

No item should be left untouched. From textile goods (draperies and bedding) to furniture and food, it is necessary to evaluate every item that could have been in the vicinity of the fire. Even if a belonging doesn't necessarily look smoke damaged, it should be inspected—confirming its safety and cleanliness.

Create an inventory

After determining which items should undergo fire content cleaning, decide on a cleaning process for each item. There are three options we utilize for fire content cleaning. Cleaning items onsite in the home, taking items off-site to a warehouse cleaning facility or taking items to be dry cleaned. If it is determined any items will need to be taken to a facility or a dry cleaner, this is called a "pack out" and the restoration company technicians will carefully pack up items to be cleaned. It is very important that a detailed inventory is created of the items that are removed from the home, including information about the condition and location of the items.

If it's determined there are items that can be cleaned onsite, those will be moved to the cleaning area—usually the garage or basement. It's important to leave the transporting of smoke damaged items to a professional crew because items could be more fragile or likely to tear or break. Additionally, if any items are not salvageable by a fire content cleaning and should be discarded, a record of everything thrown away should be kept. An inventory of all discarded items is essential to receiving compensation when filing an insurance claim.

Clean the affected items

Once the items are evaluated and recorded, the restoration team will begin the fire content cleaning process. There are a variety of advanced industry cleaning products and systems to take advantage of to professionally clean and restore smoke or fire damaged items.

Whether onsite at your home or in a warehouse cleaning facility, the restoration team will gently remove soot and smoke damage from each restorable item by hand. Typical fire content cleaning services include:

- Cleaning of all soft goods, including garments, pillows, drapes, bedding, carpet and upholstery
- Cleaning of all electronics, appliances
- Drying and restoration of documents
- Art Restoration
- Cleaning of bookshelves, shelving, furnishings and light fixtures

The type of cleaning method and products used depends on the item in question. Some of the cleaning methods to remove stains and smell include:

- **Hand washing and drying:** Items are carefully cleaned by hand. Care is taken to use dry methods with water-sensitive items.
- **Ultrasonic cleaning:** Ultrasonic tanks are used to clean certain items. Some items that might be cleaned ultrasonically are blinds, collectibles and other smaller contents.
- **Furniture and upholstery cleaning:** This requires specialty equipment, products and technicians trained and certified in furniture restoration.

Dealing with fire and smoke damage can be daunting, time-consuming and stressful—especially when it comes to a tragic or unexpected fire. Your family's life and daily routine may be displaced and disrupted, due to this very stressful event. You'll want to hire a restoration company that can also work with insurance agents to help you file claims and restore items within your budget.

3. What to Do If Caught in a House Fire

Raging flames ripping through your home – a terrifying sight we hope you never have to experience! But the reality is that thousands of residential fires occur in the U.S. every year! The causes vary from cooking accidents (#1) to heaters, cigarettes, washers and dryers, BBQ grills, candles and more. Here are tips to escape a fire if one ever occurs in your home:

- Use a fire extinguisher – but only if it's safe. Try to extinguish only small fires in their early stages. DO NOT attempt to put out any fire if it threatens your safety. Fires can increase in size and intensity in seconds, blocking exit routes and creating a toxic atmosphere.
- Scream to alert others in the house. Don't rely on smoke alarms alone to warn others. They can malfunction or have low batteries. Get yourself and your family members out as quickly as possible.
- Follow your fire escape plan and fire drills you've

practiced. Take the safest escape route and stay as low as possible to avoid inhaling smoke and deadly fumes. Cover your nose with a shirt or damp towel.

- Don't waste time picking up valuables. It usually takes less than 30 seconds for a fire to get out of control. A few seconds can be the difference between life and death. Most valuables are replaceable. You're not.
- If smoke is coming through cracks or under a door, don't open it. Touch the door and doorknob with the back of your hand to check if it's hot. If so, find another way out (door or window) to avoid flames and smoke on the other side. Never sleep in a room without more than one means of escape. A legal bedroom requires two exits, usually a door and a window.
- If you're able to open a door but heat and smoke pours into the room, stay in the room and close the door. If you can open it safely, stay low and follow your escape route. Close doors behind you to prevent the fire from spreading.
- If there's no safe exit (for example, from an upper story), stay in the room and seal the door and air vents with sheets or duct tape to prevent smoke from entering. Then call 911, open a window and yell for help. Wave a bright piece of cloth or use a light so that the firefighters notice you. Children should never hide under a bed or in a closet as that

makes it harder for firefighters to find them.

- If your clothes catch fire, remember to "stop, drop and roll" to put out the flames. Cover your face with your hands while doing so.
- Do not use elevators. If the power goes out, you could end up trapped inside the elevator, which in a fire could turn into an oven you can't escape. Always use the stairs.
- Once you're out, go to the assigned meeting place and stay there! Never reenter a burning building under any circumstances. Let firefighters, who have the necessary training and equipment save others and as much of your property as possible.

4. How to Keep Your Appliances from Going up in Smoke

If you've ever had your power go out after a storm, didn't it feel as if you had suddenly been thrust back to the dark ages? That's because homes today are filled with electric lights, appliances and gadgets that make our lives easier and provide us with entertainment. We usually don't think much about them until they no longer work, but statistics show that we should because appliances do contain a level of danger.

According to the National Fire Protection Association (NFPA), there were 339,500 home fires reported in the U.S. in 2019 (3000 in Chicago alone). These resulted in 2,770 deaths,

12,200 injuries and $7.8 billion in direct property damage. Of these, approximately 44,880 fires, 440 deaths and $1.3 billion in damages were caused by electric appliances and wiring.

Modern home appliances are safer today than they were a generation ago. Older appliances can pose a fire hazard because they may lack modern safety protections. But new appliances have more electronic bells and whistles than ever before, making it possible that bad wiring or electric components could go bad. The fact is, most appliance fires are caused by human error. The following are appliances with a history of fires and the actions you can take to have fewer issues.

Threats from common appliances:
Ovens

This appliance is the number one culprit. While grease fires on the stovetop are common, many issues can also cause an oven fire. While the oven helps contain flames if a fire starts, it can still spread to other parts of the home. Being aware of the common causes of oven fires can help you avoid this situation.

Sometimes it's the appliance itself that's to blame for a fire. Electric ovens have heating elements that can malfunction and cause sparks, which can lead to a fire. So, keeping your oven in good repair is a must. Typically, it's user error, like when an overfilled pan bubbles over and lands on the heating element. Baking greasy foods can cause the fat and grease to splatter on the heating elements as well, igniting a fire. It's always best to cover food and use a baking sheet when possible.

Never leave food unattended. Always set a timer to remind yourself of food you have cooking in the oven. Lastly, clean the inside of your oven regularly! When food debris and grease builds up, it can catch on fire.

Dishwashers

Have you ever opened your dishwasher immediately after it finished cleaning and gotten a face full of steam? That's because a dishwasher contains heating elements that dry your dishes. These heating elements get wet, heat up and cool down each time the dishwasher is run. Old or faulty elements can start a fire. So, never start a dishwasher before leaving your house. While it's nice to return home to clean dishes, it's not worth the risk.

Dryers

The most common cause of dryer fires is failure to do a thorough cleaning. Because a lint trap won't catch every bit of fuzz from clothes, lint can gradually build up and catch fire in the heating element or exhaust duct. Although it looks harmless, lint is made of flammable material. Because the fibers are so fine and short, they are essentially like kindling— lots of dry, easily ignited bits collected into one big clump.. Experts say that keeping your lint trap clean is just part of the safety cycle.

Microwaves

According to Bob Schiffmann, a 50-year veteran of the microwave industry and president of the International Microwave Power Institute, microwave fires usually start for the same reason that oven, stovetop or grill fires do: "It's simply due to [the food] overheating." Food-based fires in a microwave almost always happen because someone overestimated or entered the cook time incorrectly.

There are three other ways that dangerous microwave fires can begin. First, the power supply can short out and burn the components inside the house. Second, a power surge can trick the microwave into turning on, and it may run continuously until somebody notices and turns it off. There are reports of this happening with several brands–if this happens to you, unplug it immediately. Finally, some parts could be prone to catching fire when overheated.

Pay attention to guidelines

Many user-related causes of appliance fires are caused by carelessness, distraction or haste. And sometimes it's just ignorance. With appliances, we too often take the "set it and forget it" attitude and that's a mistake. "Most people do not follow the recommended installation, use and care of their appliances," says Ken Canziani, IAAI-CFI, senior fire investigator at Unified Investigations & Sciences, Inc. in Sacramento, CA. "Many issues or fires can be prevented if people are aware of and follow the manufacturer's recommended guidelines."

5. How to Prevent Puff Backs in Your Home

If your fireplace begins spewing smoke into your home's interior, this can become a huge disaster. When that occurs, it may be the result of a puff back. This could occur only once per season or it may happen every time you start a fire.

The results of puff backs are terrible. The smoke can damage all surfaces it touches. A foul odor permeates the environment while the air becomes dangerously contaminated with carcinogens and carbon monoxide. Additionally, smoke particles lodge in curtains, clothing and carpeting.

The good news is that fireplace back puffs are preventable. But what causes them?

Cause: Creosote buildup

Creosote is a byproduct of fireplace smoke. It builds up inside a fireplace flue every time the fireplace is lit, growing thicker and thicker. The creosote causes your chimney to generate more smoke than can be exhausted, allowing the smoke to travel the path of least resistance–back into your home.

Cure: Hire a chimney sweep

A CSIA-certified chimney sweep can inspect and identify creosote accumulation. If it's a problem, you'll need to have your chimney swept, which will remove creosote buildup and restore your chimney to its peak working condition.

Cause: Lack of air supply

While a well-insulated home is more energy efficient, a tightly-sealed home could actually "suffocate" your stove or fireplace, resulting in negative air pressure inside. This could cause the fireplace to release smoke into your home. Fire needs oxygen to burn and a tightly sealed home will limit the flow of air into the fireplace.

Cure: Introduce air flow

Before lighting your next fire, simply open a window. Back puffing should discontinue if the issue was caused by an inadequate air supply.

Cause: Obstructions

If your chimney is blocked, it'll restrict airflow and smoke will build up in the flue until it's exhausted through your fireplace or stove. Bird and wasp nests built inside a chimney can restrict its airflow, along with balls and tree branches.

Cure: Clean the chimney

The National Fire Protection Association recommends that you have your chimney, fireplace and vents inspected and cleaned annually, regardless of whether back puffs occur or not.

Cause: Unsuitable firewood

You may be trying to burn wet wood which can produce more smoke than usual. To burn efficiently, the fire needs to first burn off any excess moisture within the wood. The higher the moisture content of the wood, the harder it'll be to burn.

Cure: Use seasoned wood

Wood needs to be dry to burn efficiently. Wood that's freshly cut is high in moisture content, which is why wood needs to be dried out (known as seasoning) for 12 to 18 months before it's ready to be used on a fire without causing smoke issues.

Sometimes, a badly built fireplace can cause smoke problems. All aspects of a fireplace, such as its opening size, smoke chamber, smoke shelf, damper size and chimney height, must be built without design and construction flaws in order to prevent smoke buildup. When your fireplace pours smoke into your home, the resulting damage can be significant.

6. Holiday Fire Prevention

While the holidays are a fun time to celebrate family and togetherness, they're also a time of increased fire hazards that beg some mindfulness of fire prevention measures. Cooking and celebrating without the proper precautions can lead to a house fire, a tragedy that has caught many unsuspecting homeowners off guard during the holiday season

How do I prevent my oven from catching on fire while I'm cooking?

- Fire prevention starts by ensuring your oven is clean before using it

- Don't leave cooking food unattended
- Put a cover on food that might splatter
- Keep an eye on your timer

How do I prevent my mantle from catching on fire from holiday decorations and candles?

- Consider using battery operated candles
- Make sure you don't hang paper ornaments over open flames
- As long as flames are ignited, be sure to monitor your mantel
- Increase fire prevention by keeping decorations far away from open flames

What steps should you take to handle fire damage restoration?

Though we always encourage adequate fire prevention before disaster strikes, sometimes the unthinkable finds a way to wreak havoc on plans anyways. In the event of a holiday fire emergency, call a certified restoration company that can handle structural cleaning and content cleaning for homes that have been affected by smoke or fire damage.

7. Avoid Fire Damage From Holiday Lights and Decorations

Wintertime is magical indoors and out. Lights go up, carolers roam the streets and people are generally a little nicer than usual. Unfortunately, the risk of fire damage and the demand for fire restoration services also increases during the holiday season with the use of lights, Christmas trees and additional electrical stress. In addition to potential damage and disaster in the home, bodily injuries involving holiday decorations have been steadily increasing over the past few years. The last thing anybody wants is a holiday emergency that turns into a tragedy.

We have a few tips for avoiding the need for fire restoration so you can keep your home safe and enjoy the splendor of the season:

Check each set of lights for damage. Make sure your decorative lights are free of broken sockets, bare or frayed wires, and that all connections are tight and well-fitted. Also make sure that your lights have passed the strict requirements of and have been tested by nationally-recognized laboratories.

Use the appropriate extension cord. Indoor extension cords are not meant to hold up to the weather and elements they are exposed to outside. Lights and extension cord will both be marked with labels that specify whether or not they can be used outside. Be sure to use the appropriate outlet to avoid the need for fire restoration services.

Keep burning candles within sight. This tip applies to everyday use as well as during the holidays. Keep a close eye on candles, and make sure to extinguish them before you go to bed or leave the house. Only burn candles on stable surfaces that are heat-resistant and clear of other items that may catch fire, such as trees, curtains, furniture and paper decorations.

Buy the freshest tree you can find. Dry, old trees are much more likely to catch fire, especially with the added heat from all the decorative lights placed on it. When buying a live tree, make sure the needles bend instead of breaking, and that they don't fall easily from the branches. To elongate the life of your tree, distance the evergreen from fireplaces and heat vents so that the tree doesn't dry out too quickly. Keep an eye on the water levels in the tree stand and don't block any exits or doorways with the tree.

Do not burn wrapping paper. The large amount of paper and the mixture of materials used in wrapping paper may cause fires to take off quickly and burn intensely. The last thing you want is fire damage in your home from out-of-control flames caused by wrapping paper! Check with your local recycling company to see when and where wrapping paper can be recycled, or reuse it for various craft projects at home.

Remember, just because a label on an item says that it is fire-resistant does not mean that it is not able to catch on fire. The label "fire resistant" just means that it will take longer to become fully engulfed. Be especially careful with items that have fringe, such as the rug placed under a Christmas tree.

8. After a Fire in Your Home: What to Save, What to Toss

One of the hardest tasks to deal with after a fire is deciding what you can keep and what to toss. Many objects are obvious losses, but others may leave you unsure whether they're salvageable or not. You want to save money yet you also need to stay safe. So, the following are some tips on how to handle some of the more questionable items that may have been exposed to fire and smoke.

Food

Throw out all food that's been in contact with smoke and/or firefighting chemicals, including fresh produce, meat, poultry, fish, eggs, opened containers, food packaged in cardboard, foil, paper, plastic, cloth, screw-topped jars and canisters, and any foods stored outside the refrigerator that were exposed to smoke or fumes.

Some canned goods may still look good on the outside, but heat damage can re-cook the ingredients in the can. This activates bacteria that causes food spoilage, making them unhealthy to eat.

But won't foods that were in a refrigerator or freezer be safe? Sometimes seals on those appliances aren't air-tight and smoke can leak inside to damage food. If the electricity went out during the fire for more than two hours, then it's likely spoilage occurred so all items should be discarded.

Medicines and cosmetics

The Center for Drug Evaluation and Research (CDER) says the effectiveness of drugs can be destroyed by high temperatures from a fire. If you think your medicines have been exposed to excessive heat, consider replacing them. The same is true if they've come into contact with fire-fighting extinguishing chemicals.

As for cosmetics, high heat can change their composition without showing any visible signs. They could end up damaging hair and skin. Plus, they can absorb the toxic fumes that go along with all fires, which is not anything you want to put on your skin.

Clothing

Clothes, bedding and other fabrics can often be salvaged after a fire with proper cleaning and disinfecting. However, if anything is burned, throw it away. Use even stricter judgment when considering your child's or baby's clothing as they're more susceptible to any leftover toxic residue.

But what about clothes that were packed in plastic bags and stored inside of drawers and closed closets? Aren't they safe from smoke residue and odor? No. Rapidly expanding air during a fire easily penetrates clothing even when plastic covers are used to protect them. As the air inside the home cools down and fresh air begins to circulate, garments covered by plastic with the odor inside are not subject to the normal airing-out process. This allows the malodors to thoroughly penetrate the garment.

To add to the problem, the plastic itself will attract and

retain odor to a considerable degree and so must be removed and disposed of ASAP. Never try to salvage any possessions that could put your health at risk. When in doubt, throw it out!

9. Eight Fire Safety Tips for People with Disabilities More than 43 million Americans have a disability.

Besides the other myriad of challenges they face, they also have a greater risk of starting a fire or getting hurt in one due to decreased mobility, health, sight and hearing that may limit a person's ability to take the quick actions necessary to escape during a fire.

Dealing with physical limitations

Many actions individuals can take to protect themselves from the dangers of fire may require help from a caretaker, neighbor or outside source. To overcome their unique challenges in emergency situations, disabled ones, along with their caregivers, need to create a safety plan specific to their needs.

Eight fire safety tips that can help people of any disability (physical, auditory, visual or mental):

- Install smoke alarms in every sleeping area and every level of your home. Test the alarms monthly by pressing the test button and replace batteries each year. If you can't reach the test button, ask someone to test it for you.

- For the hearing impaired, install smoke alarms and alert devices made specifically for people who are deaf or hard of hearing. They detect the sound of smoke alarms and flash strobe lights to alert you. Those hard of hearing can also opt for smoke alarms that emit a loud, low-pitched sound alert. Additionally, use vibrating pillows and a bed shaker that wake you up when a fire alarm sounds and keep a telecommunication device for the deaf (TDD) phone in your bedroom close to your bed.

- Always be vigilant when cooking. The kitchen is where most fires caused by people with disabilities start. Always supervise the oven or stove when cooking and use a timer. Have a fire extinguisher located nearby that's reachable and be trained on how to use it.

- Live on the ground floor. Whether you live in an apartment building or a multi-story home, you should arrange to live on the first floor. By doing so, you'll be able to escape quickly and more easily in case of a fire.

- Discuss and practice your fire safety plan with your family, friends, building managers and/or neighbors. Practice your fire escape plan with your service animal if you have one.

- Let your local fire department know about your

condition and explain your needs. They can perform a home fire safety inspection and suggest escape plan ideas at your request.

- If you use a walker or wheelchair, make sure you can easily get through your doorways. If possible, design your home around your disability. Widen the doorways and install exit ramps to make an emergency escape easier.
- Always keep a cell phone on or near you to call 911 if a fire or other emergency occurs.

Your home is where you should feel safe and secure, but often danger occurs when we forget to pay attention to the simple things that could easily prevent a disaster. These risks are much more dangerous for people with disabilities, who have special needs and unique challenges in emergency situations. However, with the right planning and preparation, you'll help keep yourself and loved ones safe when a crisis occurs.

10. Fire Dangers Don't End When the Flames Are Dowsed

One of your worst nightmares has occurred: you've experienced a fire at your home. Once the firemen leave, your first inclination may be to go inside the structure to see what you can salvage and start the cleaning process, but cleaning up after a fire is much more complicated than regular cleaning. It's also very dangerous, because once the last flame has been snuffed out, the dangers from a fire continue.

Soot hazards

Since fire destroys all materials, the soot that covers everything you touch and that you kick up in the air after a blaze is full of toxic substances. That's why the highly trained professionals wear heavy duty personal protection equipment (PPE) on fire mitigation jobs until all the soot is removed. Here are some of the poisons found in the soot and ashes of a building fire:

- Mesothelioma (cancer) causing asbestos fibers from building materials
- Carbon materials can produce carbon monoxide, ammonia and nitrogen oxides
- PVC can create hydrogen chloride, phosgene (used as a chemical weapon during World War I), dioxin, Refrigerant-40, bromomethane (a pesticide), etc.
- Hydrogen sulfide and sulfur dioxide (poisonous gases)
- Petroleum based items can produce formaldehyde, acrolein, furfural, cresols and other harmful chemicals
- Even wood smoke releases more than 100 chemicals also found in cigarette smoke

Children, the elderly and those with weakened immune systems are predominantly at risk when exposed to smoke and soot. Its adverse effects have been known since the 19th century when the British Parliament passed the Chimney Sweepers Act 1875, partly in response to its association with cancer—the first ever occupational health legislation.

Professionals not immune

A study conducted by the National Institutes of Health has found that firefighters have higher rates of cancer than the general population due to exposure to smoke and toxic soot because many did not wear the proper gear. In fact, The International Association of Firefighters says cancer is now the leading cause of death among firefighters.

"It was never really something we thought about when I first started 32 years ago. It was a badge of honor to come out with all your gear dirty," said Peter Silva Jr., a former firefighter. "If you didn't wear your mask in there you were a strong, aggressive firefighter, and if you went in with your mask on, you were kind of ridiculed at times."

Protection

Because of these dangers, incident commanders are now ordering firefighters to keep their masks on until they're away from the smoke and soot and washed down by decontamination teams on the scene. Once back at the station, they're being told to change into a second set of turnout gear while industrial washing machines clean the dirty outfits.

If fire professionals take this issue seriously, shouldn't you? The advice of Boston Fire Commissioner, Joseph Finn, is priceless. He says, "I've buried way too many friends over my 33 years. Too many friends... so I tell them, 'Think about your wife, your husband, your boyfriend, your girlfriend before you take that mask off your face.'"

11. Fire Extinguisher Safety Tips That Can Save Your Life

There are many preventative measures you can take to reduce the risk of fire damage to your home, such as smoke detectors, an evacuation plan and a fire safety kit. If a large fire breaks out, you'll need to call the fire department and wait for help, but certain small fires may not require outside assistance and can be put out with a fire extinguisher. But before you do, the following is information that you need to know.

Find your fire extinguisher

It's smart to know the location of your fire extinguisher(s) before a fire breaks out and you're stuck without it. Everyone who resides in your home needs to know where it is. Your fire extinguisher should be hanging on the wall in plain sight so that no one has to go searching for it in an emergency. Kitchens, laundry rooms and garages are the best places in a home to store them because heat sources and flammable chemicals are most present in those rooms.

If you don't own a fire extinguisher, buy one immediately. They come in a variety of sizes and prices and should be affordable by all. If you are a renter in Illinois, for example, your landlord is required to provide a fire extinguisher on each floor of your apartment complex if the building is more than three stories or in each apartment/unit.

Inspect your fire extinguisher

It is important to regularly inspect your fire extinguisher to make sure it's in working order because the worst time to discover that it isn't is during a fire. Check the inspection tag for the date your fire extinguisher was last inspected to judge if it needs another one. To work correctly, the gauge's needle should only point to the green "charged" zone. Otherwise, it needs to be recharged

If you find cracks in the hose, or if it's too brittle to bend easily, get it replaced. Be sure the pin is securely tied to the extinguisher with a safety tether. Other damages, such as corrosion, dents and leaking, will require replacement of the unit.

How to use your fire extinguisher

Everyone in your home needs to know how to use a fire extinguisher before an emergency. Go to a safe, isolated, outside area to practice. It is highly recommended that you use the P.A.S.S. technique to operate your fire extinguisher:

1. PULL
2. AIM
3. SQUEEZE
4. SWEEP

First, pull the pin and break the tamper seal on the fire extinguisher. Second, aim the extinguisher nozzle low at the base of the fire. Third, squeeze the handle to release the extinguishing agent. Finally, sweep back and forth until the fire is completely out. (If you have any doubts in your ability to operate a fire extinguisher during a fire, evacuate the premises instead.)

Cleanup and recharge your fire extinguisher

Since the extinguishing material in most fire extinguishers is a dry chemical, you can use a vacuum cleaner to remove any remaining residue once the fire is out. The extinguishant is similar in texture to sand, so you should be able to remove most of it. Once the loose residue is picked up, use a damp rag to scrub up whatever is left. Be sure to keep your hands protected because the chemical can potentially damage your skin.

Even if you only discharged a little of the fire extinguisher, the cylinder still needs to be replaced or refilled. If you don't, it won't be able to help protect you if another fire breaks out. Call your landlord or a local, licensed fire protection company to recharge it.

12. Don't Be a Victim of Carbon Monoxide Poisoning

Not very long ago, a couple fell asleep in their car that was parked in a garage. They not only left the vehicle running but were also operating a kerosene heater due to the extreme cold. Needless to say, they died due to carbon monoxide (CO) poisoning.

Although that sounds like a sad and absolutely avoidable way to go, every year at least 430 people die in the U.S. from accidental CO poisoning and approximately 50,000 others are forced to visit the emergency room because of it. CO deaths occur regularly and the stories are heartbreaking.

The reason why CO is dangerous is because it interferes with the oxygen-carrying capacity of blood. Being colorless, odorless and tasteless, people can be overcome without any warning. Symptoms caused by exposure to CO include low energy, headaches, dizziness, weakness, nausea, vomiting, chest pain, confusion, visual impairment and (obviously) death.

CO is found in fumes produced by furnaces, kerosene heaters, vehicles "warmed up" in garages, stoves, lanterns, gas ranges, portable generators or by burning charcoal and wood. CO from these sources can build up in enclosed or partially enclosed spaces, poisoning people and animals.

When a storm knocks out power, many rely on portable generators to keep the lights on until electricity is restored. Fred Henretig, a senior toxicologist at the Poison Control Center at the Children's Hospital of Philadelphia, says he and his colleagues have been attempting to raise awareness about proper portable generator use for years, but carbon monoxide poisoning cases unfailingly surge after each big storm.

"So what people tend to do — not always but it's not unheard of — is just set it up like right next to the open garage door and they think, 'OK, that's going to work fine, it will blow out,'" Henretig explained. "The exhaust will blow out, but the trouble is, you can't always account for different drafts and how things get vented around."

Research suggests that in natural disasters, carbon monoxide poisoning from portable generators has the potential to take more lives than the disasters themselves. A study tracking confirmed deaths related to Hurricane Irma in Florida, Georgia and North Carolina in 2017 attributed 16 fatalities to carbon monoxide poisoning and 11 to the storm itself.

Here are ways you can you protect yourself from CO poisoning, whether a disaster has occurred or not:

- Purchase and install at least one carbon monoxide detector on each floor of your home, including the basement.
- Change the batteries in your CO detector every six months.
- Have gas, oil or coal burning appliances serviced by a qualified technician every year.
- Keep vents and flues free of debris so as not to block ventilation lines.
- Never leave a vehicle's motor running while parked in an enclosed or partially enclosed space, such as a garage.
- Never run any gasoline-powered engine within 20 feet of an open window, door or vent where

exhaust can seep into an enclosed area, or inside a basement, garage or other enclosed structure, even if the doors or windows are open.

- Never use a charcoal grill, hibachi, lantern or portable camping stove inside a home, tent or camper.
- If your CO detector goes off during or right after a disaster, leave your residence immediately and call 911. If you feel light-headed, dizzy or nauseated and suspect you may have CO poisoning, seek immediate medical attention.

13. Lingering Tobacco Odors Are Still a Health Hazard

Have you ever rented or bought a home that had been totally renovated yet you could still occasionally smell cigarette smoke? That's because after years of being subjected to smoking, even the structural elements of a building can be saturated with tobacco odor leaving nasty smells in all rooms, not just the one where someone smoked the most.

What tobacco smoke leaves behind

Cigarette smoke deposits are yellowish-brown, gluey substances that stick to all surfaces in a home, making it hard and time-consuming to remove. If you've ever cleaned windows or walls that have sustained large amounts of cigarette smoke, you've easily seen this residue.

As stated by the American Lung Association, cigarettes

contain over 7,000 chemicals (40 of which are linked with cancer) that not even the stoutest air purifiers can eliminate from your home. But it's not just an odor dilemma.

How does tobacco smoke affect your home?

Studies conducted by San Diego State University show that third-hand smoke that emits from walls, carpets and curtains can have a substantial impact on our health. Deadly and volatile composites from tobacco smoke build up in drywall and in soft furnishings. Children are particularly at risk of diseases triggered by exposure to the toxins from third-hand smoke.

"There's a big illusion that when tobacco smoke disappears, we're safe," said SDSU psychology professor Georg Matt, director of the resource center. "Unfortunately, some of the most toxic compounds cling to surfaces. They get embedded in carpets, they coat walls, they penetrate into walls. They become part of the indoor environment."

Smoking not only adversely affects those exposed to smoke, but it also produces malodorous elements that stick to all surfaces of the area where smoking has occurred. The yellowish-brown gunk produced by smoking bonds to walls, furniture and plastics, and may forever change their appearance. Cigarette smoke also infiltrates odor-absorbing objects, such as insulation, carpets, upholstery, bedding, clothes and more.

Additionally, a building's HVAC system transports smoke odor and chemicals all over the structure. That means that over time, the buildup of dust and debris inside HVAC ducting absorbed those odors and will need to be cleaned out. Additionally, the entire ducting system will need to be thoroughly cleaned and sanitized.

How professionals remove tobacco smoke odor

There's no magic formula that will eradicate these residues and smells. Covering up odors with air fresheners only works briefly and might pose health risks. Furthermore, trying to conceal tobacco smells with a fresh coat of paint without first eliminating the source won't successfully eliminate the odor. Within a short time, smoke residue will begin seeping through the paint and will once again spread offensive odors throughout the room.

The only successful way to eliminate tobacco residue and odor is by the very thorough cleaning and then sealing of all structural surfaces. We start tobacco smoke removal by cleaning all surfaces, using deodorizing agents to eliminate the very minute particles of tobacco smoke. Once we've finished cleaning all visible surfaces, we use specialized equipment, such as hydroxyl generators and/or ozone generators, that destroy the odor molecules that are unreachable (such as inside walls or joints).

The next step consists of using a sealant to lock in the very last stains and odors. After that, surfaces will be prepared to paint, refinish or apply new coverings. You want to make sure that all surfaces are sanitized and treated to make sure odors stay away from you and your possessions.

14. Grill Safety

When the weather heats up in the month of June, nothing signals the start of summer quite like the scent of grilled burgers, hot dogs and veggies wafting through backyards. But good eats come at the risk of tragedy if you don't mind your grill safety.

When a hot summer afternoon rolls around, the Restoration By Simons team loves outdoor cookouts as much as anyone else. But what we don't love as much is the increase in fire and smoke damage calls we receive after big grilling days, especially since most fires caused by grills can be avoided by following a few key safety tips. Here's the low-down on the steps you should be following to make sure food is the only thing your grill chars:

Exercise good grilling habits

- Set your grill up a safe distance away from other objects. We can't tell you how many times we've been called on a job that involved grill flames consuming sides of houses because the grill was too close! Also watch out for overhangs, sheds, garages and other potentially flammable items.
- Never use your grill inside, in a tent or under an outdoor awning. Not only does this cause fires, but it also puts you at risk for carbon monoxide poisoning if you have a gas grill.

- Avoid getting burned by lighting your grill using special long-length matches or lighters.
- This goes without saying, but never leave an actively burning grill unattended. Make sure to let your grill cool completely before covering or storing it.
- Clean your grill thoroughly to reduce flammable buildup inside.

Understand the intricacies of charcoal grills if you use one

- Be careful not to overuse the charcoal—you should add only enough to cover the bottom of the grill. If you use too much, it could cause ashes and sparks to become airborne.
- Use care when storing your extra charcoal. We recommend keeping it in an airtight metal container, far away from sources of flame.
- Buy starter fluid specifically meant for charcoal and only apply it to cold coals. Don't add extra fluid once the grill is actively burning to mitigate the risk of high flames and uncontained fire.
- Don't clean the grill or empty your ashes until they have fully cooled. When you dispose of them, we suggest dumping them on garden soil. Avoid storing or disposing of them in a garbage can, or worse, leaving them on your deck. Ashes can still cause a fire, even after they've cooled.

Be smart when using a gas grill

- Open the lid before lighting the grill to allow oxygen to escape and limit the risk of fire or explosion.
- Regularly inspect your grill's gas line and tank fittings for leaks by brushing soapy water around those areas. If you see bubbles emerge, there could be a leak somewhere and you'll need to replace any faulty parts before using the grill.
- Never store spare gas cylinders under a stairway in your home. Instead, keep them upright and outside, at a safe distance away from other structures.
- When you turn off your grill, use the controls first and then close off the gas line at the tank. This will ensure that excess gas escapes safely.

Summer afternoons are meant for cookouts, family and fun—not fire tragedies. Follow our grill safety tips to keep your home safe this summer.

15. Use Extension Cords Safely to Prevent the Need for Fire Restoration

When used correctly, extension cords are super handy tools for delivering power right where you need it. However, if they're not used as intended, they can cause a fire and necessitate the need for fire restoration.

The Electrical Safety Foundation International (ESFI) offers the following tips for staying safe from electric shock and electrical fires:

- Never substitute extension cords for permanent wiring.
- Do not overload extension cords.
- Do not use an extension cord rated for indoor usage outdoors. They are a safety hazard if they become wet.
- Do not run extension cords through walls, doorways, ceilings or floors. If the cord is covered, heat can't escape, which can result in a fire hazard.
- Don't use an extension cord for more than one appliance.
- Use extension cords with polarized and/or three-prong plugs.
- Buy only cords approved by an independent testing laboratory, such as Underwriters Laboratories (UL), ETL-SEMKO (ETL) or Canadian Standards Association (CSA).
- A heavy reliance on extension cords is an indication that you have too few outlets to address your needs. Have additional outlets installed where needed.
- Never use a cord that feels hot or is damaged in any way. Touching even a single exposed strand can give you an electric shock or burn.
- Make sure the extension cord is rated for the products to be plugged in.

When used correctly, extension cords are super handy tools for delivering power right where you need it. However, if they're not used as intended, they can cause a fire and necessitate the need for fire restoration.

16. Hoarding Greatly Increases the Risk of Fire Damage

According to the National Fire Prevention Association's Public Education Division, more and more fire departments are seeing serious home fires, injuries and even death as the result of compulsive hoarding disorder. In addition to the filth, damage and pests that can make a hoarder's home unsafe, the increased risk of fire makes it all the more important for compulsive hoarders to have their homes professionally cleared out and cleaned up.

Hoarding is the persistent difficulty of discarding or parting with possessions, regardless of their actual value, according to the Anxiety and Depression Association of America. Hoarder behavior usually has devastating effects–emotional, physical, social, financial and even legal–for both the hoarder and family members. For those who hoard, the quantity of their collected items sets them apart from other people. Commonly hoarded items may be newspapers, magazines, paper and plastic bags, cardboard boxes, photographs, household supplies, clothing and food. As you can see, many commonly hoarded items can easily feed a fire.

There are many reasons that hoarding has become a fast-growing issue for firefighters and hoarders alike. They include the following:

- Hoarding can be a fire hazard. Many occupants

die in fires in residences that have become home to a serious hoarding situation. Often, blocked exits prevent escape from the home. Also, many folks who are hoarding are injured when they trip over things or when materials fall on them.

- Responding firefighters can be put at risk due to obstructed exits, falling objects and excessive fire loading that can lead to collapse. Hoarding makes fighting fires and searching for occupants far more difficult.
- Those living adjacent to a hoarder can be quickly affected when a fire occurs due to intense smoke and fire pouring from the hoarder's home.

If you or a loved one are ready to take the big step toward cleaning up the hoarding situation in your home, Restoration By Simons offers respectful and non-judgmental help, working tirelessly, professionally and compassionately to clean your home and return it to a safe and happier condition.

PART 3:

INSURANCE

It's no secret that investing in home insurance is a vital part of the buying/leasing process, but how much do you really know about your home insurance coverage aside from the basic necessities (like what plan level your landlord requires or how much that plan costs per month)? Without reading the fine print, it's hard to know exactly what your homeowners insurance covers and if you're getting the full value out of your policy.

Trust us, after years of working with insurance companies, we totally get it. Home insurance is a tough subject, but we believe it doesn't have to be, so we've included a guide to serve as a valuable resource for homeowners with surprising things that homeowners might be covered for. We hope that you will use these guides to better understand your homeowners' insurance policy and more successfully advocate for yourself and your living space.

1. The Most Common Causes of Property Damage for Homeowners

Homeowners insurance covers many surprising things that we would have never guessed! However, spoiled food and slander are not examples of losses that are frequently filed for at homeowners' insurance agencies. Between 2012 and 2016, the most common causes of property damage for homeowners based on the claims made were: water and freezing damage, wind and hail damage, theft, fire and lightning damage, bodily injury, medical and credit card damage (fraud or theft).

THE MOST COMMON CAUSES OF PROPERTY DAMAGE FOR HOMEOWNERS

Homeowners Losses by Claims Frequency from 2012-2016 (Claims per 100 House Years)

Water Damage & Freezing:
1.99 claims

Wind & Hail:
2.38 claims

Other Property Damage:
.74 claims

Theft:
.37 claims

Fire & Lightning:
.31 claims

Bodily Injury & Property Damage:
.09 claims

Medical Payments & Other:
.04 claims

Credit Card & Other:
Less Than .01

2. How to Read Your Homeowners Insurance Policy

Did you know that the vast majority of U.S. homeowners are insured, but most of them don't fully understand their own policy? Of course this is the case, with a variety of different insurance carriers, agents and policies, understanding what a policy does and does not include coverage for can be a daunting task. But the good news is there are additional steps homeowners can take to be better informed, aside from picking up the phone and calling their insurance agent.

Here at Restoration By Simons, we've made it our goal to ensure clients and consumers are well-versed in their specific homeowners' insurance policy. We can't tell you how many times our clients have been shocked to find out their insurance doesn't include coverage for something they assumed it did, and we would hate for that to happen to you! In general, our professionals advocate for a call to your homeowners insurance agent, because they can give you the fastest and most direct answers. *But*, we also recognize that sometimes a phone call isn't the best place to start. For example, if you don't know what questions you should ask because you don't know how to read your policy to find the information necessary to formulate questions. That's why we created this simple 3-step how-to guide to help you understand how to read your homeowners insurance policy.

1. Talk the talk

Sometimes, reading over an insurance policy can feel near impossible if you don't understand the lingo. In order to better understand your policy, there are a few key terms you'll want to get familiar with:

- Replacement Cost: The full amount it costs to replace your home.
- Actual Cash Value: How much the insurance company values your home after it accounts for depreciation of its value.
- Insured: Who is covered under your policy? It's a good idea to make sure your pets and family members fall under this category, too.
- Deductible: The specified amount you must pay in the event of a loss before your insurance company will help cover costs.

Declaration page: In general, most insurance companies use forms and contracts that look pretty similar. Pretty much across the board you'll have a declaration page, which will be near the top of the contract. Usually, at the head of the document, there will be some indication that you are looking at the declaration page. This part of your contract is probably the best place to start if you're trying to understand your policy better, since it summarizes your coverage all in one place. It will include the policy number, policy period, your name and address, the address of the insured home, name of your mortgagee, your coverage types and policy limits, deductible amount for the policy, home-rating information, your discounts and the premium amount.

2. Parse through your property coverage

After the declaration page, homeowners' insurance policies generally have two parts. Section I includes information about your property coverage, while Section II details your liability coverage. We recommend you look at the property coverage section next. There will likely be three subsections, dwelling, personal property and loss of use. Keep in mind that between the protection you have under these three sections, you want to make sure you are covered for rebuilding your dwelling if its structure is damaged, replacing personal property, additional living expenses and the cost of personal claims. You can discuss the coverage amounts you see listed under property coverage with an agent to see if you are under-covered with your current policy.

3. Look for your personal liability

Once you've reviewed your property coverage, find Section II (personal liability) and figure out how much liability you're covered for. This section protects you against lawsuits for property damage or personal injury that you or your family cause to other people. You'll want to double-check to make sure this portion of your policy covers the injured party's medical bills, legal fees and any damages awarded to the injured party. These things should be clearly spelled out in Section II of your policy document.

We know that taking the time to understand what's in the physical contract you signed when you bought homeowners insurance isn't a fun or easy task, but it's a necessary evil. It's important to glean as much valuable information from your policy documents as possible before you pick up the phone, so that you are better equipped to ask your insurance agent questions. Understanding the language and knowing where the different sections are located will also help you better process the answers your agent gives you. The professionals here at Restoration By Simons recommend setting aside two hours to sit down with the heads of the household and review the policy one weekend.

3. Four Things Not Covered by Homeowners Insurance

It's no secret that homeowners insurance is pretty confusing. From the wide variety of insurance carriers to the wide range of coverage offered by different plans, it can be hard to understand the coverage you need versus the coverage you have. We want to focus on surprising things your homeowners insurance probably does **not** cover!

We believe in full transparency when it comes to insurance, which is why we've used our expertise to bring you this down-and-dirty guide to five sneaky things that probably aren't covered under a standard current policy.

1. Earthquakes and floods

Standard home insurance policies usually won't cover earthquakes or floods, but many homeowners are unaware of this fact and end up paying huge bills out of pocket. For many cities in the US, flood coverage is especially important with all the heavy spring rains we've been having in recent years. You'll definitely want to consider discussing coverage options for disaster restoration with your insurance agent because, oftentimes, flood and earthquake coverage can be added onto your policy as an endorsement. If not, you can probably purchase coverage for these disasters separately.

2. Burst pipe repairs

This one is super sneaky. You see, if a pipe bursts in your home, the water damage restoration is usually covered under standard home insurance policies. However, the actual cost of *pipe repair or replacement* is generally not. Depending on how many pipes burst and for what reasons, that could be a pretty big out-of-pocket bill you'll have to take on. Another thing to note here is that if the burst pipes were caused by negligence (meaning, you didn't repair them when they should have been or didn't take steps to resolve freezing pipes), your insurance company could also deny your claim for water damage coverage.

3. Nuclear accidents

The possibility of a nuclear accident might sound far-fetched, but, honestly, we think it's a more likely scenario than people give it credit for. According to the Federal Emergency

Management Agency, about three million people in the United States live within ten miles of an operating nuclear plant. If you're one of those three million, the bad news is that you're probably not covered. With the very real threat of an accident that could cause uninhabitable levels of radiation, it's best to proactively talk to your insurance agent about your options.

4. Sinkholes

When it comes to sinkholes, it's the same story as earthquakes and floods—damages caused by them will almost definitely not be covered by a standard homeowners' insurance policy. There are two exceptions to the rule, though. If you live in Florida or Tennessee, sinkholes are covered under "catastrophic ground cover collapse." Talk to your insurance agent to find out if this coverage is offered through their company because sometimes this coverage can be hard to obtain.

Insurance coverage can be difficult to understand, but our goal is to help homeowners like you, become an expert on your own policy. Now that you know what your insurance may not cover, read on to learn what homeowners insurance does cover. Then, we recommend that you take the next step and give your agent a call. The best way to understand your specific coverage is to ask proactive, straightforward questions.

4. Thirteen Surprising Things You May Not Know You Are Covered for

What does homeowners insurance cover?

Let's face it, homeowners insurance is overwhelming. People spend hours researching and selecting a carrier and plan, but still don't fully understand their coverage. In fact, when people call the professionals at Restoration By Simons for their various restoration-related needs, they have many questions about what their insurance does and does not cover. So, what does homeowners insurance cover? When it comes to coverage for "personal property," things get complicated, and unless someone has a background in insurance, they likely don't realize the full potential of their policy.

At Restoration By Simons, we believe in demystifying homeowners insurance to help our clients get the most out of their coverage. That's why we've done a ton of research and combined it with our 20 plus years of experience dealing with insurance agents to bring you this ultimate guide to 13 totally surprising things your home insurance may cover.

1. Mandated upgrades

If your home is out of compliance with a newly-passed city ordinance, your insurance "ordinance coverage" clause might help you bring your home up to code. Sam Simon, our managing director, has also seen upgrades covered for clients under an "HO-3" policy. He says, "It's a clause in standard basic homeowner policies that provides coverage for most city ordinances that require bringing a property up to code after a covered loss. For example, in vintage Chicago homes that experience fire and smoke damage, the policy would provide not only coverage for the damage, but also extra coverage to upgrade old two-prong electrical outlets to the now standard three-pronged outlets. It helps homeowners meet municipal ordinances at the same time as it makes the home safer and increases its overall value... a bonus for the homeowner."

2. Spoiled food

After a power outage that renders a refrigerator useless for many hours or days, you'll probably have to throw out hundreds of dollars' worth of spoiled food. If you file a claim with your home insurance carrier, you could find yourself covered up to $500 depending on the reason for the power outage.

3. Slander/libel

Let's pretend you slandered someone or published libelous materials about a company and they took legal revenge and sued you. Before you pay your legal costs outright, take a look at your home insurance policy. We're not saying we recommend slandering others, but you wouldn't be the first to file a claim for this!

4. Student property

If you have (or will eventually have) a kid at college, you might not have to worry so much about the rampant theft some campuses experience. Even though your student takes his or her things out of the house with them to college, your home insurance policy could cover their belongings as "off-premises personal property" in the case that they are stolen. However, according to Carolyn Streett, a sales consultant at Dakota Insurance Group, this coverage can be difficult to obtain, "If the student is living in an off-campus residence, they might not be covered and should instead inquire about renters' insurance. I always recommend the insurance buyer call their agent and explain that their child is away at school, explain where they are living and ask how that affects the personal property coverage." Other requirements for claiming stolen student property could include full-time student status and verification that your student is under 26 years old.

5. Falling objects

Standard home insurance policies cover damage caused by falling objects. We have seen clients use their policy to cover damage to property, contents, vehicles and personal injury caused by objects such as asteroids, meteors and falling satellites. Your policy will also commonly cover damage caused by a falling tree or even falling ice from an airplane, which is more common than you think. If you own a property next to or near a high-rise building, odds are your property will be struck by a falling object at some point.

6. Additional living expenses

This category is ambiguous and encompasses a variety of things, from natural disaster relief to weather damage repairs. Common "additional living expenses" people are covered for include repair costs for damages caused by snow or burst pipes and hotel costs if your home is uninhabitable after a storm. Additionally, our clients often find their policy covers spikes in electricity bills they may experience during a restoration job (our equipment uses a lot of watts!).

7. Away-from-home accidents

If you accidentally break someone's leg in a pick-up basketball game while you're on vacation, try filing a liability claim. Random accidents that happen outside your home might be covered by your homeowner's insurance if no vehicles are involved.

8. Gravestones

The only thing worse than vandalism is vandalism done to a loved one's gravestone. Gravestones are personal property, so if you're the primary caretaker, you can probably use your home insurance to cover the damages. "Depending on the carrier, grave markers could also be covered," says Carolyn Streett of Dakota Insurance Group.

9. Fire department bills

According to State Farm agent Brent Becker, fire department visits can result in a bill. "Fire departments can charge you for their service," he says. "But your home insurance policy might help pay for it depending on the reason for the visit."

10. Dog bites

According to the CDC, approximately 4.5 million dog bites occur in the United States each year, and 1 in 5 of those will become infected. If Fido mistakes Aunt Susie's leg for his favorite chew toy and you are served a lawsuit, your wallet could avoid a hit. Most policies have $100,000 to $300,000 of liability coverage for injuries caused by pets, in addition to medical coverage for the bitten party. One-third of home insurance claims are actually for dog bites, so your insurance agent will be a well-versed resource.

11. Identity theft

In the age of digital data, identity theft is a real and serious threat. If the unthinkable happens to you, your home insurance policy might help restore your peace of mind faster. Some policies will cover lawyer fees, lost wages and fees charged for loan re-applications if you were rejected based on inaccurate credit bureau information. However, you probably aren't covered under your standard policy, warns Carolyn Streett of Dakota Insurance Group. "Usually, carriers have identity theft insurance available for purchase as an add-on to your policy," she says. "Make sure you speak with your insurance agent before you assume this coverage is automatic."

12. Volcanic eruptions

If you don't live in Hawaii, are volcanic eruptions enough of a threat to include with standard home insurance coverage? Some insurance carriers think so — including State Farm. According to Brent Becker, "Earthquake coverage is available under endorsements, while flood coverage must be purchased separately, but if lava destroys your home, you'll be covered under most policies without any special add-ons."

13. Riots/terrorist attacks

If rioters loot your shed or a terrorist attack (like an explosion or fires) damages your property, your home insurance may cover it. There are, however, some specific restrictions for most policies when it comes to terrorism.

What does homeowners insurance NOT cover?

Dog bites? Volcanic eruptions? Betcha didn't see that coming! We know, some of the things people have gotten their home insurance to cover seem a little out of left field, but, believe us, it's been done. And if you file a claim in response to any of the above events, you might save some money. One disclaimer, though—you'll have to weigh the money you might get back by filing a claim against the increase in your premiums you'll risk with most insurance carriers. In general, it might not be worth making claims that result in payouts of less than $500. But hey, it's a pretty cool party trick to know home insurance covers spoiled food!

It's also important to remember that not all home insurance is created equal and what kinds of things you'll be able to obtain reimbursement for is likely dependent upon the terms of your plan. Insurance is definitely not black-and-white, and carriers will provide different levels and scopes of coverage. We recommend further discussion with your insurance broker or agent, who can adequately educate you on what must be added to your policy based on your coverage goals versus what you are already covered for.

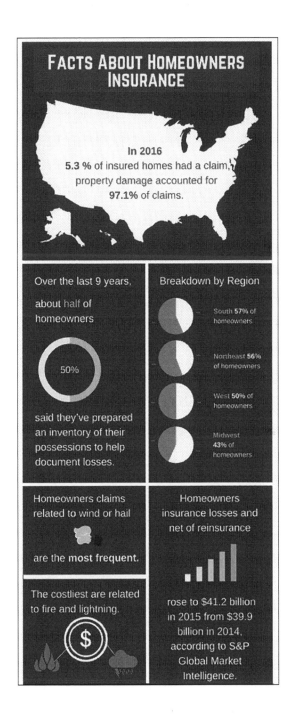

FACTS ABOUT HOMEOWNERS INSURANCE

In 2016
5.3 % of insured homes had a claim,
property damage accounted for
97.1% of claims.

Over the last 9 years,

about half of homeowners

50%

said they've prepared an inventory of their possessions to help document losses.

Breakdown by Region

South **57%** of homeowners

Northeast **56%** of homeowners

West **50%** of homeowners

Midwest **43%** of homeowners

Homeowners claims related to wind or hail

are the **most frequent.**

The costliest are related to fire and lightning.

$

Homeowners insurance losses and net of reinsurance

rose to $41.2 billion in 2015 from $39.9 billion in 2014, according to S&P Global Market Intelligence.

5. Common Factors Affecting Your Insurance Rate

What factors are affecting your insurance rate? Common factors are crime, weather, home values, your neighborhood, building materials of your home, your dog breed, type of stove, marital status, insurance score, proximity to a fire department, proximity to a coast, credit history and your claims history!

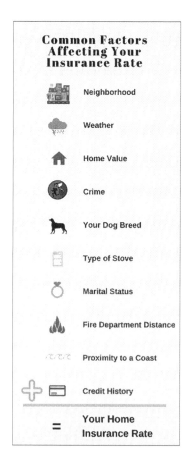

6. Five Things You Need to Ask Your Insurance Agent

Insurance policies and carriers vary widely, leaving homeowners with a lot of misinformation and a really big headache. At Restoration By Simons, we know that clients are often under-informed when it comes to what their policy does and does not cover, and we've made it our mission to help consumers demystify the insurance process. We understand that talking to insurance agents can be intimidating, especially when you are unsure of what questions to ask (or when you don't realize questions you should be asking). That's why we created this list of five questions we recommend asking your insurance agent to better understand your coverage.

1. Is my home covered for full replacement cost?

This is probably the most important question you can ask! You'll want to find out if your home is only covered for market value, or if it's covered for the amount you paid up front. In some cases, it might only be covered for your loan value. If it's covered for anything other than the amount it sold to you for, you're likely under-insured and you'll want to explore additional coverage options with your home insurance agent.

2. How much coverage do I have for the contents of my home?

Usually, contents are covered as a percent of the overall

value of the home. For example, some policies will cover contents up to 50 percent of the value of the home, others might go as high as 70 or 75 percent. You can discuss your particular percentage with your agent, and possibly add more coverage in the case of contents whose combined value exceeds your current policy coverage.

3. Am I covered for earthquakes?

You'll want to find out if you are covered for earthquake damage because many policies do not include it as a standard. The same goes for coverage on flood damage. You can discuss the need for these types of coverages with your insurance agent, who will have location-based statistics and can advise you whether or not to add it to your plan.

4. Am I covered for water damage caused by sewer overflows or water pressure from below ground?

Similar to earthquakes, water damage from these specific sources is usually not covered on standard homeowners' insurance policies. But that doesn't mean they aren't real problems you might face! In our opinion (after working hundreds of water damage jobs in the last year alone), it's definitely worth a conversation about adding this coverage to your current policy.

5. How much is my policy's deductible?

The deductible is the amount of a loss you are responsible to pay, while your premium is how much you pay up front for your policy. Finding out your deductible amount is vital to understanding your policy and that way there won't be any surprises if you file a claim. Your agent can also help find the right balance between premium and deductible prices (usually as one goes down, the other goes up).

7. Homeowners Insurance vs Renters Insurance

In general, you either *own* a home, or you're renting the property or unit on which you currently live. Rental units are obviously not owned by the tenant, but that doesn't mean insuring the property as the renting tenant is any less important than if you were to own your own property! In fact, as a rental tenant, it is arguably more important to make sure your coverage stacks up, since you will likely have another party holding you accountable, instead of going it alone.

Here at Restoration By Simons, most of our clients are property owners, but we definitely don't want to forget about insurance tips for rental tenants. We know that rentals come in many different shapes and sizes, with landlords whose policies vary across the board, and sometimes that makes insuring a rental property even more difficult. We want to help make the rental insurance process a little less confusing, so our professionals talked to industry leaders to bring you this guide of the differences between renters insurance and homeowners insurance and why those differences matter if you're the rental tenant who needs to find adequate coverage.

In general, we'd say that renters insurance gets treated a little bit like homeowners insurance's overshadowed little brother. Insurance agents report that people tend to think one of two things about renters insurance. One, that renters insurance is a lot like homeowners insurance (even to the point of being a different name for the same thing!); or two, that renters insurance only covers personal property, such as damages to or theft of valuables. The reality is that these misconceptions are simply untrue, so let's check them at the door! Renters insurance is completely different from homeowners insurance, although sometimes the two do work in tandem between the landlord and the renter. To help set the record straight, here are the three biggest differences between homeowners insurance and renters insurance:

1. Structural coverage

Perhaps the biggest and most obvious difference between the two types of insurance is that the actual, physical structure of the home is covered under a homeowners policy, while renters insurance doesn't cover the building in which the renter resides. More specifically, homeowners insurance covers the home as well as any other building structures on your property. If you're a renter, since you don't technically own the building, your insurance won't cover damages due to, say, a fire or flood. Instead, the landlord you rent from should have homeowners insurance that covers structural damage in the event of those kinds of disasters. As a renter, it's a good idea to double check with your current or potential landlord to make sure they are properly covered. However, a good thing to note is that as a renter, if a fire is your fault (perhaps you left the stove on by accident), you could be held responsible. The liability portion of your renters insurance will probably cover for these types of damages, but it's always a good idea to double-check.

2. Renters insurance usually costs significantly less

Another obvious difference between renters insurance and homeowners insurance is the cost. In general, renters insurance costs much, much less and is pretty much considered affordable across the board. Usually, renters can get insured for less than $20 a month. Homeowners insurance, on the other hand, could put a big dent in your wallet. Understandably, since it insures a whole home structure instead of just a unit and homeowners generally have a higher number of high-value belongings.

3. Requirements for tenants versus homeowners

Homeowners and renters alike are usually surprised to find out that while homeowners insurance is pretty much required upon purchase of a property, renters insurance isn't always a requirement. By law, landlords can ask that you do get renters insurance upon signing a lease, but more often than not, they don't. In fact, according to Allstate, only 45% of renters carry renters insurance. But of course, this doesn't mean you *shouldn't* get renters insurance on your own to cover your belongings and help you if you're held liable for a fire accident.

8. Flood Insurance

When is water damage not water damage? When your insurance company gets involved! You see, although losses caused by water can be identical no matter the source of the water, insurance companies differentiate between what they consider water damage, flood damage and sewer backup. So, to make sure that ALL assets of your home are totally covered, you'll need to have coverage for all types of claims.

Flood insurance

Although it seems counterintuitive, the standard property insurance policy does not cover damage caused by floods. You'll have to purchase a separate policy for that. To be labeled a flood, insurance companies follow the legal definition set by the Federal Emergency Management Agency (FEMA) that it's a "general and temporary condition where two or more acres of normally dry land or two or more properties are inundated by water or mudflow." Flood conditions are caused by such things as overflowing rivers, heavy rains, overflow of tidal waters and mudslides.

Water damage insurance

The good news is that in many home insurance policies, water damage is part of your standard policy. The main distinction from flood insurance is that water damage occurs before the water hits the ground. Some examples of such a claim would be:

- Water damage resulting from the extinguishing of a fire
- Soaked floors following a storm that broke windows
- A leaking appliance
- Accidental cracking, burning or bulging of a steam, heat or AC system
- Frozen pipes that have burst
- A leaking roof

Sewer or water backup insurance

These problems are possible caveats to what's considered flood or water damage. Most policies will not cover damage caused by a sewer or water backup (e.g., from a leaking in-ground swimming pool, koi pond or other subsurface water feature on your property). You'll need to purchase separate insurance coverage as an add-on to your homeowner's policy to be covered. Their payout limits usually vary between $5,000 and $25,000.

(Please note: Even if the water came from beyond your property, such as a pipe maintained by the city, your insurer still won't cover it unless you purchase the special coverage outlined above.)

If you have questions about any of this, contact your insurance agent. If your home is located on a flood plain, your agent will likely recommend that you purchase additional flood insurance to reduce your financial risk.

9. Five Tips for Choosing Home Insurance

It's no secret that buying a home is a huge time commitment and emotional investment, but the decision making process isn't over when you sign a contract with a real estate agent. What most people don't understand is that choosing a home insurance can be just as tough as choosing a home in some cases. The insurance industry is as fragmented as ever, with a dizzying array of carriers and plans available to homeowners. It's no wonder that 5% of homeowners go uninsured, according to the Insurance Information Institute.

No matter how confusing it is, home insurance is a necessary evil. The professionals at Restoration By Simons are with you and we want to share some pointers that other clients have found helpful. With our top tips for selecting home insurance, you will be more prepared to sift through your options and make an informed decision that works for your family.

Determine a budget that works for you

We recommend insuring your home for its replacement value instead of the price you paid for it. Think about how much it will cost to purchase materials and hire a crew to rebuild or repair the home if it is damaged, and make sure your home insurance policy reflects this cost. You should also discuss the repair cost increase you might expect given inflation with your insurance agent.

Take into account the home's history

You should know the nitty gritty ins and outs of your home before you begin shopping around for home insurance. Find out the claims history from the previous owner so you know if there are any recurring problems you'll need to cover with policy add-ons. We like to tell clients that they need to evaluate what they want from an insurance policy and if there are any unusual things they'd value in a policy based on the history of the home. You'll also want to understand if there are any problems or aspects of the home that could make it harder to get insurance or raise your premiums. Gather as much info as possible about the electrical and septic systems, foundation construction and lifespan of the home.

Find out if there are price cuts available to you

We totally agree that there's nothing more important than insuring your home and making sure you are covered in the case of an emergency so safety and peace of mind can be restored as soon as possible. But we also want to keep in mind that insurance policies can be expensive and even though it's hard to put a price tag on your peace of mind, the reality is that people often don't have money to throw around on overpriced insurance policies. The good news is that there are often price breaks depending on your geographical location, proximity to a professional fire department, home's age and number of installed safety features (like fire alarms). You might also save on insurance if you bundle your home and car insurance with the same company, and that might be an option worth exploring if you're looking to save some money.

Don't go with your first option, get multiple quotes

The number of choices for insurance carriers and plans might make your head spin, but it's always better to brave the multitude and get multiple quotes from different carriers for different levels of coverage. Having too many options is bad, but so is having too few. If you jump on board with the first insurance plan you find, you risk settling for a plan that doesn't do what you need it to at the price point you are targeting. We always tell our clients the energy and time investment to talk to multiple carriers is so worth it in the end. You are much more likely to be happy with your insurance policy when you set yourself up to make a good decision.

Understand the policies available to you

While you should absolutely spend the time getting multiple quotes and talking to a variety of carriers, your efforts will be much less effective if you don't also take the time to truly understand each policy and its fine print. You'll want to read through the entire policy and clarify things with the insurance agent as needed. Don't be afraid to ask tough questions—their job is to help make sure you are well-informed. There's nothing wrong with taking the steps to make your policy as transparent as possible

PART 4:

CLEANING & DISINFECTION

Your home is supposed to be a haven for relaxation, recuperation and escaping the pressures of the world. Unfortunately, we wind up bringing home some of the world and its germs via our dirty hands, shoes, clothing and phones.

As of this writing, we are in the "after times" of a pandemic. Thus, even if your home looks clean, it could still be hiding contaminants that could affect your health. Making sure you are cleaning and disinfecting your home is more crucial than ever. In doing so, it's important to also be sure you know the difference between cleaning and disinfecting, and are using them both to combat viruses and protect the health of your family.

Medical experts agree. Dr. Michael Schmidt, professor of microbiology at the Medical University of South Carolina and chair of the American Society of Microbiology's Council on Microbial Sciences, says that the best way to protect your family is to be sure you're cleaning and disinfecting your home's trouble areas. This includes high-touch surfaces and the hard-to-reach places that you might not even see or recognize. He also has some helpful tips for recognizing the difference between cleaning and disinfecting and using both processes to your advantage to disinfect your home from coronavirus.

So what's the difference between cleaning and disinfecting? Cleaning shouldn't be confused with disinfecting. Here are the key differences: When you clean, you remove germs, but don't kill them. When you disinfect, you *kill* the germs to rid surfaces and your home of them. This difference is important because though you might clean surfaces well, small amounts of germs and bacteria are left to grow, which can perpetuate the spread of viruses. Cleaning is the process of wiping down surfaces and areas of the home to slow the spread of germs and dirt. This includes countertops, doorknobs, light switches and common surfaces. You can do this twice a day with a microfiber cloth dampened in a solution of hot water and an all-purpose cleaner. Cleaning eliminates the spread of germs. Disinfecting is the process of killing germs and bacteria using specific approved cleaning solutions/agents.

1. Can You Clean with Only Water?

For everyday cleaning, wouldn't it be terrific to be able to use just water? You would probably be able to free up an entire cabinet devoted to cleaning products. Plus, you would remove the danger of accidental ingestion by children and unintentionally mixing up a dangerous chemical cocktail that could emit poisonous fumes. But is it realistic to believe that water alone could clean your home?

John Owen is a senior household analyst for a market research firm. He says, "People are increasingly equating a clean home with a healthy home and a healthy family, but at the same time there's also concern about the cleaning product ingredients. So, for these consumers, they still want their homes clean, but they're looking for alternatives."

Additionally, a test conducted by consumer advocacy group CHOICE discovered that some of the popular cleaning products sold in supermarkets aren't as effective as we think. They found that about 50 percent of those they tested weren't noticeably different from plain water.

It turns out that for daily light cleaning, using only water, even hard water, with a microfiber cloth can be effective. Microbiologist Dr. Michael Schmidt says microfiber, which is smaller than a human hair, is good at trapping dust, and even bacteria and viruses. "It's this frizzy end at the end of this very small fiber that facilitates the pickup of bacteria and viruses from surfaces," Dr. Schmidt said.

If someone is ill or when it comes to cleaning up kitchen

counters that have been in contact with raw food, Dr. Schmidt says to "use a disinfectant and good old elbow grease to make certain that that material is gone."

However, before you start spraying and wiping everything down with water, there's another factor to consider: many items and materials in your home should never be cleaned with water only as it could harm or even ruin them. Let's discuss a few.

Wood furniture and hardwood floors

Why? - Water can damage the finish and leave areas of discoloration. It can also cause wood to swell, split and crack.

How to clean: Use a high-quality furniture polish or lemon oil to shine and protect wood furniture. If hardwood floors still look dingy after dusting, deep clean them with any pH-neutral, wax-free and petroleum-free cleaner. We do not recommend using white vinegar and water because it is acidic and has drying effects on wood. Additionally, vinegar has a very strong odor that many people find unpleasant and "unclean."

Leather

Why? - Water can leave streaks and spots on leather and after a while can cause it to crack.

How to clean: Use either a leather conditioner cleaner or lightly dampen a cloth with lukewarm water, apply a small amount of hand soap to the cloth and clean the leather by wiping with the soapy cloth, working in circular motions, then buff with a dry cloth. Don't rinse the soap off—it'll help condition the leather.

Brass and silver

Why? - Using water to untarnish brass and silver pieces will only lead to more tarnish. Most household brass and silver has been treated with a lacquer or sealant and eventually water will remove this protective barrier.

How to clean: Apply a brass or silver polish formulated specifically for cleaning and protection, or use vinegar and a soft microfiber cloth. Rinse the brass or silver piece with lukewarm water after cleaning and then wipe dry with a soft microfiber cloth.

Musical instruments

Why? - Water discolors and damages wood-based instruments and can remove protective coating from metals, causing the instrument to tarnish and rust.

How to clean: Employ only cleansers that are specifically designed for musical instruments. Contact a professional for cleaning guidance about your particular instrument.

Electronics, keyboards

Why? - Using water to clean these items can permanently damage sensitive electronic components.

How to clean: A damp microfiber cloth can remove most dirt and dust. Use cotton swabs or canned air to get into crevices around buttons and computer keys. For heavier soil, use rubbing alcohol on a clean towel. There are many electronic cleaning sprays available for purchase that are effective, just make sure to read the directions before using. You can also simply use a can of compressed air to blow out dirt from keyboards or electronics.

Soft quality fabrics such as silk, velour, velvet and suede

Why? - Water can leave spots, streaks and stains, and may lead to shrinking and pilling.

How to clean: Vacuum fabrics regularly and use a soft brush to remove surface soil. For deeper cleaning, depending on the fabric, use an upholstery cleaner, a dry-cleaning cloth or a dedicated suede cleaner.

Light fixtures and outlets

Why? – Water and electricity are a deadly combination. When they meet, they can cause shorts, sparks, electrocution and fire.

How to clean: First, shut off the power before cleaning. Then wipe with a soft cloth to remove dust and dirt. Use compressed air to blow out the interiors and never use water to clean a hot light bulb as doing so could cause it to shatter.

Brick, marble and stucco

Why? – Even materials that are hard as rock are still porous. Water may remove any protective sealant that might have been applied during construction and could damage and loosen grout and caulking.

How to clean: vacuum the surfaces regularly, use a soft brush to sweep away dust and dirt, then wipe down with a soft cloth.

Although water can clean up light soils on some surfaces, you will still need to use other cleaning strategies to help clean, preserve and protect different materials and items in your home.

2. Tips for Making Your Home Look and Smell Spring Clean

After a long, cold winter, one of the greatest pleasures is throwing open the windows and letting in warm, fresh spring air. More than likely, that first whiff of spring is probably the reason why "spring cleaning" has become part of our consciousness. We want the inside of our home looking and smelling fresh too!

Diving in and doing some deep cleaning can make a significant difference when it comes to the overall look and feel of your home. Besides regular vacuuming, dusting and mopping, let's discuss several other ways to brighten up your home and improve its air quality.

Concentrate on these areas:
Clean windows and screens

Dirty windows not only let in less light, but they show up dirt easier than most any other area of your home. With newer tilt-in windows, this isn't the chore it used to be. If you have older second story windows that require ladders to reach them, either have professionals handle it or at least make sure you have a spotter on the ground. While you're at it, clean dust and debris from your screens by brushing them with a scrap of carpeting.

Get the air ducts cleaned

There are numerous benefits to doing this. Allergies,

which usually increase in the spring, can be even worse if there's also excess dust and dirt particles floating around your home. Considering that the average American spends 90% of their time indoors, improving indoor air quality is vital.

Clean blinds and drapes

These can accumulate a ton of dust. For blinds, use a microfiber blind brush that will do the job quickly and efficiently. For curtains, remove them from their rod/hooks and throw them in the dryer with a slightly damp towel. Turn your dryer on for about 20 minutes set on the "air fluff" (no heat) setting. The damp towel will help pull off any dust or fur and the tumbling action will finish the job. As soon as they're done, hang them back up right away.

Have your carpets professionally cleaned

Rental carpet cleaners don't pre-treat pesky spots or rinse your carpets with water afterward. A systematic cleaning with high powered equipment will not only ensure cleaner carpets, but will also extend their life.

Clean the washing machine

Although you'd think it would clean itself, over time detergent residue, bacteria and dirt can build up in a washing machine, leading to musty smells and not-so-clean laundry. To clean it, fill the drum with a ½ cup of baking soda and a quart of vinegar, then run a wash cycle. (Or use tablets made for cleaning washers.) Use the hottest water setting, largest load size and the longest wash cycle. Meanwhile, between loads, always keep the lid open to allow it to dry out completely inside, reducing the chances of mildew growth.

Clean the kitchen trash can

Sure, you use plastic trash bags, so your trash can should be clean, right? Unfortunately, even after taking out the garbage, foul smells can still linger in your trash bin. Those odors have a way of drifting throughout your home. Baking soda can work wonders at preventing those smells. Sprinkle some in the bottom of a trash can or directly into the trash to help absorb stinky odors. As a bonus, baking soda is great for scrubbing out your trash can to remove odors that may have seeped into it.

Declutter your home

A home with less clutter is a cleaner home. Not only does it look neater, but there's also less surface areas for dust and dirt to collect on. One way to straighten up is by putting items back where they belong. (For instance, clothes don't belong in the kitchen and dishes don't belong in the bathroom.)

Sometimes, decluttering means getting rid of stuff. This isn't always easy to do. We get attached to our possessions. So, chucking them takes self-honesty and will power. If you haven't used (much less touched) an item in over six months, do you really need it? If not and it has some value, donate it. Doing so is not only tax deductible, but it also helps others and makes you feel good about yourself. There are many charitable organizations that accept a wide range of donations.

3. When Chemicals and Extreme Temperatures Don't Mix

Some inanimate items that don't do well in freezing weather are many of the cleaning chemicals you use. Check the labels for any freeze warnings that they may post. When some non-aerosol products freeze, the solids within the solution will fall out and can't be blended back into the mixture. When this happens, the product is basically useless and will need to be thrown out. But if water-based products freeze, you can thaw and shake them and they should be good to go.

Aerosol products work best at room temperature or warmer. Many aerosols consist of a water-based product and a solvent-based propellant. When an aerosol can is very cold, it won't dispense properly. Instead of a nice even spray, either nothing will come out (even though there's still plenty of product inside) or it'll just spit at you like an angry camel. The reason for this is that when a water-based product gets cold, it gets thick and sluggish. So, when the nozzle is depressed, what dispenses is mostly the solvent-based propellant instead of the product and you end up with a can full of a cleaning product that you'll never be able to use. This problem is easily alleviated by running a cold can under hot water for about a minute or so before using. Your best bet is to store them inside a heated building and not somewhere like an unheated garage.

Problems with aerosols also exist on the other end of the

temperature spectrum. Spray cans of cleaners, deodorant, hairspray, spray paint, etc., can explode at 120 degrees. It can get that hot inside an enclosed, uncooled building on a scorching day. The temperature inside a parked car can get up to 140 degrees on an extremely hot day and that's past what it takes for aerosol cans to explode. Never store aerosols in any place that gets hot, such as on top of a radiator, a fireplace mantle, a water heater, or near furnaces, wood stoves or space heaters.

Many carry and store hand sanitizers in their vehicles these days. Although they're unlikely to explode in high heat due to the fact that they're usually hand pumped and not used in aerosol cans, they can lose their effectiveness if they sit in a hot car. Those products contain alcohol, which, once hot, evaporates much more quickly than water. Once this happens, they lose their sanitizing properties.

Interestingly, most products sold in aerosol cans are more expensive by weight or volume than their non-aerosol counterparts. The propellant in an aerosol can may account for as much as 15 percent of the weight. Economically, non-aerosol products are more cost-effective. If you really want to save some cash, buy concentrated cleaning chemicals where you mix them yourself. By doing so, you can realize a savings from dollars per gallon to cents per gallon.

The welfare of your cleaning chemicals may not be the very first thing on your mind, but considering how much money you spend on them, they're worth a little consideration on your part.

4. Does Your Renovation Budget Include Post Construction Cleaning Costs?

If you're planning a residential project and you're not already thinking about a plan for clean up afterward, you should be. You'd be surprised how often we find that customers have forgotten to budget for or schedule a post construction cleaning until the very last minute. The problem is many customers don't realize that post construction cleaning is an important part of any building project. They don't understand that post construction cleaning is some of the most important projects a restoration company will take on. These kinds of jobs usually require a company's entire crew to be onsite for anywhere between a few days to a whole week, depending on whether it is a residential or commercial project.

We like to make sure that customers understand the level of care and commitment that goes into each of our post construction cleaning projects. We use products and equipment that meet the highest standards to remove all dust and debris properly. Some of the post construction cleanup services you'll want to look for include:

- Dusting air diffusers
- Cleaning light fixtures within the construction area
- Cleaning restroom fixtures
- Wall washing or spot cleaning walls
- Ceiling washing

- Cleaning interior windows
- HEPA vacuuming
- Cleaning carpet areas
- Damp mopping hard-surface floors
- Renewing hardwood floors
- Roto buffing ceramic tile or linoleum

For larger jobs that need further cleaning after construction work has cleared, we often bundle carpet and upholstery cleaning and hard surface floor cleaning with services. A successful cleaning process is one that maximizes efficiency while still delivering the highest level of service. Ideally, our process begins well before the construction project occurs, when a customer reaches out proactively for a quote.

Sometimes, we are asked to begin our on-site cleaning for a mid-way cleaning while construction is still taking place. This is helpful for large construction projects that generate so much debris that it creates an unsafe environment and poor air quality for workers. Cleaning periodically during construction is important so that waste is removed and dust is kept to a minimum. Most of the time, though, our on-site cleaning starts immediately after construction concludes.

There are two primary objectives during post construction cleanup. The first is to eradicate and control the dust generated by sanding and plastering before it ends up in the air ducts. The second, to remove all dust and debris in a timely manner to restore safety to the job site.

Five major steps of post construction cleaning:

1. Schedule air duct cleaning.
2. Clean all hard surfaces and fixtures, nooks and crannies, furniture, windows, doors, shelves, molding, baseboards and items in renovation space.
3. HEPA vacuum carpet, hard surface flooring and upholstery.
4. Clean flooring with wet mopping, WoodGlo Renew or roto tile buffing depending on the floor material. Repeat.
5. Dispose of all construction debris on-site according to municipal guidelines and regulations in a safe manner.

Because these jobs can be so large and costly, it's important that customers budget for them in their initial construction project plan. Customers are sometimes floored to learn the cost of their site's post-construction cleanup and are too late in the game to make room in the budget for it. Instead, they choose to DIY the cleanup or, worse, forgo it altogether. We never recommend this and we would rather see customers reach out for a quote during the planning stages of a construction project so they can budget accordingly.

Though professional cleanup services are costly, they are always one hundred percent worth it. Here are three reasons why:

- **Professional cleaning increases safety:** With construction projects, there will inevitably be debris left behind. From sawdust to nails and broken glass to stray wires, these debris present dangers to both the building crew and those responsible for a DIY cleanup. Accidents during cleanup happen more often than you might think. Hiring a professional crew trained to deal with hazardous materials will ensure the safety of everyone involved. A restoration company is equipped with better equipment than a broom and a dustpan.

- **Professional cleaning ensures debris is properly disposed of:** Most municipalities have special rules for the disposal of residential construction waste, like paint and other chemicals. In general, they must be separated, sorted and eventually delivered to a special facility for lawful disposal. It is important to work with a professional restoration company or you could face a fine.

- **A professional cleaning promotes efficiency and timeliness:** We estimate that a professional cleaning crew will likely be able to complete a post construction cleanup job four times faster than a DIY-er. Professional crews come with the necessary equipment it takes to clean thoroughly and efficiently. A quick cleanup allows you to move on to the final stages of your construction project. Plus, calling in the professionals for a quick turnaround can mean all the difference for contractors whose agreements include penalties for going overtime on the project.

5. Biohazard Cleanup – What, When and Why?

When you hear the word "biohazard," what comes to mind? Biohazards come from a number of sources, for example, emanating from traumatic events where blood, human or animal residues, chemical spills, and more are involved. They include these scenarios:

- Crime or homicide scenes
- Suicide or death
- Blood and bodily fluid residues
- Hoarding scenes
- Animal waste or remains
- Chemical/drug hazards
- irus contamination

Biohazard cleanup involves cleaning, sanitizing and deodorizing areas where such traumatic events have occurred. Cleanup after these events is a serious business that not just anyone can handle. The threats involved posed by bacteria, viruses and infectious diseases can put your health and safety at risk. Oftentimes, these pathogens are invisible, making cleanup an even more difficult task for the inexperienced.

You may think that if the police are involved, someone else will clean up the aftereffects, but the state of Illinois isn't responsible for cleaning up crime scenes. After police investigators collect evidence from the scene, it's up to the property owner to hire a biohazard remediation company. A professional cleanup team can arrive onsite only after the police have gathered enough evidence related to the crime.

Does biohazard cleanup require certification?

To become a biohazard technician, obtaining certification is not required. However, the Occupational Safety and Health Administration (OSHA) does require biohazard technicians to properly wear personal protective equipment (PPE) when dealing with bloodborne pathogens, because every time technicians handle potentially hazardous materials they're put at significant risk.

The professional company you call should employ state-of-the-art protective equipment, along with cleanup and disinfection processes that follow strict safety protocols outlined by OSHA and the US Environmental Protection Agency (EPA). Furthermore, the cleaning company should provide up-to-date bioremediation training for technicians that includes best practices, proprietary methods and safety compliance.

Biohazard cleanup process

- Begin cleanup efforts as quickly as possible.
- Remove all potentially infectious materials from the site.
- Hazardous medical waste is handled in compliance with OSHA regulations. It's then processed and sent to a licensed hazardous medical waste incinerator.
- Technicians remove porous materials like fabric and carpeting following industry standards and Illinois state regulations.

- Non-hazardous materials are either removed or decontaminated and sanitized if they are considered salvageable.
- After cleanup and sanitization, affected areas are deodorized and walls and flooring may be sealed to cover any remaining stains from the incident.

As with any type of property damage, we ensure that our actions don't worsen the sense of loss of a property owner. We strive to be exceptionally sensitive to these situations by showing extra care and compassion and do our best to understand that those involved may be emotionally vulnerable, and so treat grieving family members and other loved ones with respect and empathy.

6. Home Ventilation: How Ventilation Prevents the Spread of Viruses Indoors

From 2020-2022, people were bombarded with officials' imploring the public to wash their hands, watch your distance and wear a mask. In turn, the "three w's" have certainly helped to curb the rise of COVID-19 in some areas. But as the coronavirus is new (although it seems like it's been here forever), scientists are continuing to learn new things about it and its transmission. One main topic has become about how ventilation prevents the spread of COVID-19 and viruses indoors.

The research to this effect is definitely sound. In July, 239 scientists from 32 countries wrote an open letter to the WHO showing evidence that tiny virus droplets people expel when they cough or sneeze can hang in still air for hours, making crowded indoor spaces with poor ventilation risky for the spread of COVID-19. Then, in late August, a team of infectious-disease experts argued in a new analysis in the peer-reviewed medical journal, The BMJ, that six-feet protocols are too rigidly small and are based on outdated science and studies of different viruses. Instead, these experts now believe the evidence shows that the novel coronavirus can travel farther than six feet under certain conditions and that six feet is the bare minimum of space that should separate people, especially in poorly ventilated indoor areas.

As immunizations rolled out and residents started to return to school and work and began spending more time indoors, good home ventilation was seen as the key to prevent the spread of COVID-19 indoors. Here's how to ensure proper ventilation and stop the spread of viruses:

Keep it fresh

Trust your nose. If you walk into a room or building where the air feels stuffy and stale, turn around and leave because chances are the ventilation is insufficient. Without proper ventilation, COVID-19 and other viruses could spread indoors. Simply put, the more outside air that enters a building, the better. Bringing in fresh air dilutes any contaminant in a building, whether a virus or something else entirely, and reduces the exposure of anyone inside. "Having 100% outside air or close to 100% is a good thing," says Catherine Noakes, professor of Environmental Engineering for Buildings at the University of Leeds. "The more fresh air, the less you're running the risk of recirculating the virus through the building."

In warm weather, it's pretty easy to get a larger amount of outside air into a building by keeping windows and doors open (or cracked if the AC is on) and by putting a box fan in a window blowing out which can greatly increase the air exchange rate.

In cold weather, try micro-ventilation. This means that you just crack open one window in each room to permit a little fresh air to enter. To help keep the room warm, switch ceiling fans to "winter" mode. Most ceiling fans have a switch that reverses the blade direction. This reversal pulls the cold air up and pushes the warm air downwards.

Check the air conditioner

If a building you enter has a split air conditioner (a slim white box mounted on a wall or ceiling), the air is not likely recirculating air effectively. All air conditioners recirculate air, but smaller ones like these don't have the filtering capacity of larger, outside units.

For your home HVAC, it's recommended using a MERV-12 level filter that removes particles down to 1.0–3.0 microns as a good medium between effective filtration and likely compatibility with your existing equipment. (Note: Since higher-rate filters allow less air to flow through your furnace, it's a good idea to check if your system has a maximum MERV rating. The wrong type of air filter can force your furnace to work harder and increase the risk of it breaking down.)

Use air cleaners

Lew Harriman, director of research and consulting at HVAC consulting company Mason-Grant, and a member of the ASHRAE Epidemic Task Force, says concerning filtration, "Don't let the air conditioner carry that load. Frankly, you should have an air purifier even if you're not concerned [about airborne viruses]."

Air purifiers remove particles from the air, usually using a filter made of tightly woven fibers. They can capture particles containing bacteria and viruses and can help reduce disease transmission when used along with other best practices recommended by CDC and others. But not all air purifiers are equal.

Here are some points to keep in mind

- Your best option is a cleaner that uses a high-efficiency particulate air (HEPA) filter, as these remove more than 99.97% of all particle sizes
- Think about how powerful an air cleaner you'll need. The bigger the room, or the more people in it, the more air needs to be cleaned.
- Scrutinize the validity of the claims made by the air cleaner manufacturer. The Association of Home Appliance Manufacturers (AHAM) certifies air cleaners, so look for their verified seal.

Use a CO2 meter

Since the coronavirus is most often spread by breathing, coughing or talking, you can use this meter that checks CO2 levels to see if the room is filling up with potentially infectious exhalations. A well-ventilated room will have around 800 ppm of CO2. Higher numbers are a sign the room may need more ventilation.

Good air quality is just one way to help protect yourself, your families and coworkers. A higher air quality helps prevent the spread of viruses indoors. It is also important to consider air duct cleaning services. The EPA found indoor air may be two to five times—and occasionally more than 100 times—more polluted than outdoor air and may cause health problems. To improve the function of your air purifiers, have us clean your air ducts regularly. That way you'll be able to breathe easier, both literally and figuratively.

7. How HEPA Filters Protect You

During World War II, the Atomic Energy Commission needed a filter that would remove and trap radio-active dust particles that would pose a health hazard to scientists working on the Manhattan Project, the classified U.S. government venture that developed the atomic bomb. That's when and why the HEPA (high efficiency particulate air) filter was created.

The HEPA filter was specifically designed to protect the

human respiratory system. Because it's made of ultra-fine, glass-fiber materials, it captures microscopic particles that can pass through other filters easily. It will filter out 99.97% of the 0.3-micron particles in the air. Particles that size are nearly 300 times smaller than the diameter of a human hair and 25 to 50 times tinier than the human eye can see. But to a HEPA filter, catching a one-micron particle (1/1,000,000 of a meter) is comparable to stopping a cotton ball with a door screen.

HEPA filters are viewed as the highest form of air filtration. Hospitals, laboratories and NASA spend thousands to millions of dollars to create contamination free environments termed clean rooms that aid in eliminating nearly all foreign elements, infectious agents, heavy metal particles and other undesirable impurities. For those reasons and more, HEPA filters are extensively used.

We at Restoration By Simons regularly use air scrubbers that employ HEPA filters to aid in removing contaminants in the air of a structure. These powerful, high performance, heavy-duty units are completely safe air purifying devices.

Several times each hour, an air scrubber sucks in contaminated and dusty air from a space, draws it through several filters (including a HEPA filter) and then pumps out fresh air that's free of dust, chemicals and odors. The HEPA filter captures small particles such as mold, bacteria, asbestos, lead, dust and many other floating contaminants. Air scrubbers continuously scour the air and provide a clean, healthy and productive environment. That's why our company utilizes them on jobs such as:

- Water damage restoration
- Renovations
- Cleaning and disinfecting
- Hoarder clean up
- Mold remediation
- Sewage remediation
- Fire damage restoration
- Odor removal

Don't confuse heavy duty air scrubbers with simple air purifiers. Purifiers are intended to be used inside a home when it's occupied. So, they're engineered to run quietly and to fit in with their surroundings. Although some contain HEPA or other high efficiency filters, they are much weaker than air scrubbers and are only effective in small areas.

8. Is Bleach a Safe Disinfectant?

Chlorine-based bleach has been around for a long, long time. It was invented in Europe in the late 18th century, and many consider it the be-all and end-all solution to their cleaning needs. With growing concerns about the coronavirus (COVID-19), people are using bleach as a disinfectant at increasing rates. With this increased use, we've heard households wondering, is bleach a safe disinfectant? While bleach can be dangerous in some instances, the good news is that the Centers for Disease Control and Prevention (CDC) recommends a diluted bleach solution for disinfecting your home for COVID-19. (But make sure your bleach isn't past its expiration date or it'll be ineffective against the virus.)

The CDC recommends using the following solution on suitable hard surfaces:

- 5 tablespoons (1/3 cup) bleach per gallon of water
- 4 teaspoons bleach per quart of water

Be sure to let your mixed solution set for at least one minute before using it to disinfect.

When is bleach not safe?

For some soft or hard surfaces, the CDC does say that bleach is dangerous — and instead recommends that you disinfect with an EPA-registered household disinfectant.

Even though in bleach in general is a safe disinfectant, it's important to remember that it can do your house great harm if you're not careful. This is because bleach contains chlorine, which is a dangerous chemical. Here are ten reasons why bleach isn't always the safest choice for cleaning your home:

- Chlorine lacks detergency – in other words, it contains no wetting agents that allow it to penetrate soils, so surfaces must be pre-cleaned before chlorine will effectively kill germs. This is a two-step process that requires more time.
- Chlorine is very caustic to human tissue. It can produce irritation and burning on your skin and could cause blindness.
- Chlorine reacts with other chemicals to create toxic

byproducts and gases. For instance, when bleach mixes with ammonia, it can form chlorine gas, causing cellular damage in nasal passageways and lungs. The accidental mixture of these two products has resulted in death. It's also incompatible with products that contain hydrochloric acid, phosphoric acid and acetic acid (vinegar).

- It may harm your children. After using, bleach remains on surfaces and continues to emit fumes. Recent studies show that children who have been exposed to bleach in their homes are more likely to suffer from respiratory illness. In addition, various studies have linked the use of bleach in a household to a higher prevalence of asthma and allergies.

- Using bleach can hurt your pets. Your cleaning products can stay on a pet's paws or fur. Since cats and dogs often lick themselves, they may ingest harmful chemicals. Due to their tiny size, birds can become sick upon inhaling only a small amount of the fumes. Bleach poisoning in pets can result in vomiting, convulsions and sometimes death.

- Bleach can kill mold, BUT it depends on the surface the mold is on. Mold grows on both porous and non-porous materials. When dealing with mold on non-porous materials such as shower tiles, tubs, vinyl window trims, countertops, etc. you can use bleach to kill the mold and disinfect. But using bleach to remove mold from porous materials like drywall and wood can actually accelerate mold growth rather than killing it! When bleach is used on porous materials, the chlorine is left on the surface and only the water component of the bleach is absorbed into the material, aggravating the situation as this provides more moisture for the mold to feed on, where it may then produce allergens and irritants.

- Chlorine is extremely corrosive to metal surfaces and can permanently discolor countertops. It can also damage floor finishes, requiring them to be stripped and recoated, which is an expensive process.

- Chlorine discolors fibers and colored surfaces. Carpets, upholstery and clothing are just a few of the materials that may be damaged.

- Chlorine bleach's disinfectant power is rapidly inactivated by contact with organic matter, such as blood, saliva, tissue, urine, feces, dirt, etc. Chlorine is also weakened by sunlight.

- Diluted chlorine bleach quickly loses its effectiveness, is unstable and can lose its disinfectant qualities very rapidly compared to other, more stable disinfectants.

Safe and effective alternatives to bleach

If you're looking for a safer alternative to bleach, here are some ideas:

- Baking soda and white vinegar – they're non-toxic

and non-corrosive. Use them to freshen fabrics, eliminate grease and clean glass. (Not effective against COVID-19).

- Rubbing alcohol – effectively cleans plastic surfaces of electronics. (A concentration of around 70% will kill COVID-19.)
- Hydrogen peroxide – it's non-toxic and can be used to disinfect household surfaces. Unlike bleach, hydrogen peroxide is safe to use around food products. (Effective against COVID-19.)
- Soap and warm water – the basics! It'll clean just about anything in your home and won't present any health risks. (Follow up with a disinfectant to be effective against COVID-19.)

Bleach is a safe disinfectant—usually. It's a cheap chemical to find at the store, making it a great purchase for families on a budget. Although bleach products may be a bargain, you owe it to yourself, your family and coworkers to use a product that truly cleans, thoroughly disinfects and is safe to use. We're not saying not to use bleach to disinfect your home, but definitely consider if it's safe in specific instances. Don't be afraid to use alternatives that are just as effective, if you are worried about it! Sometimes, DIY disinfecting with bleach just isn't an option.

9. Should Green Cleaning Products Be Used to Disinfect?

Natural and eco-friendly cleaners that don't harm people, animals or the environment have become important focusses for consumers worldwide. Consequently, many people are now choosing cleaning products that are categorized as green, non-toxic or natural. While most of these products are acceptable for everyday cleaning, you should be aware that nearly all do not have the required disinfection abilities to kill harmful viruses and diseases, like COVID-19.

Cleaners and disinfectants—What's the difference?

When your objective is to disinfect surfaces against infectious diseases, the best way to discern which cleaners are also disinfectants is to verify the product has an EPA registration number on the label. If one does not exist, then it isn't a tested and registered disinfectant. It'll be safe to use the product to clean up dirt and grime, but it won't disinfect against viruses and disease.

What does the EPA recommend?

The EPA's task is to safeguard human and environmental health. Based in Washington, DC, the EPA is responsible for establishing standards and laws that promote exactly that.

The EPA is focused on the elimination of contagious viruses and diseases and has developed a searchable database of disinfection products available to the public.

These have been laboratory tested and are confirmed effective against the coronavirus and other infectious diseases. These disinfectants typically use harsh synthetic chemicals like quaternary ammonium to kill germs. Therefore, this list contains few green cleaners, with the exception of citric acid.

Some research has revealed that citric acid, an organic compound that occurs naturally in citrus fruits, has antibacterial and antimicrobial properties—enough to eliminate some types of bacteria, mold and mildew. Nonetheless, it's primarily considered a cleaning agent or microbial at best. When it comes to disinfecting (killing) harmful viruses, most natural or "green" ingredients, such as citric acid, are not as effective as their EPA-registered counterparts. All except one.

Benefect is a green, plant-based botanical disinfectant product and is EPA tested and proven 99.9% effective in killing the coronavirus without any risk to animal and human health or the environment. It's now an EPA List N registered disinfectant. The downsides are that it is very expensive and can be hard to get during the pandemic.

If Benefect is not available and you want to use a natural cleaner that has been tested by the EPA that may have a lower risk of causing asthma, irritation, hormonal disruption or carcinogenic effects and pose the least threat among chemicals in their class, you can pick a product from the EPA's Safer Choice List. This list should not be confused with the EPA's List N of coronavirus-killing disinfectants. The Safer Choice is a list of products that are fine for routine cleaning, but aren't disinfectants for coronaviruses.

10. Why Hoarding Cleanup Should Only Be Done by Professionals

With the popularity of reality TV shows in recent years, like Hoarders and American Pickers, it's easy to see that hoarding is a bigger problem than most of us ever thought about. When this is an issue with family or friends, we may feel the need to help them. But when cleaning up these homes, more is involved than just taking out the trash.

Most people who hoard on an extreme level have emotional and mental health problems. They are fiercely attached to their collections and may compromise their own safety and their relationships with others just to hold on to those items. When the well-being of the home's occupants is in danger, cleaning up a hoarded home is necessary. When you do, it's best to call in professionals who handle such cases regularly.

Hoarding dangers

Here's a list of hazards that come with cleaning up a hoarder's home and why you shouldn't try to handle it yourself:

- **Fire:** This is the main danger in a hoarded home because much of the clutter consists of flammable materials, such as boxes, magazines, old mail and paper trash. Fires may occur when these types of objects cover a heat vent or damaged wires. Moreover, clutter blocks residents from escaping from a fire and first responders may not be able to navigate a hoarded home to rescue the residents.

- **Injuries:** These can occur due to falls or trips as there's very little room to walk. Piles in a hoarded home can reach as high as ceilings, which can collapse and cause injury. Someone may even get trapped under falling debris and contents.
- **Diseases:** Pests like rats and cockroaches can infest a hoarded home, increasing the chance of infecting people with diseases from their droppings or bites. With animal hoarders, the prospect of disease gets even worse as owners fail to pick up after their pets. Sometimes those animals die, but their bodies are never removed, which intensifies the sanitation problem.
- **Mold:** Due to the lack of proper airflow in a home because of stacks of trash, mold may develop. Additionally, water damage from a clog or water leak, even a small one, mixed with organic material is the perfect recipe for mold growth. Hoarders also have difficulty throwing away food and plates of half-eaten food may sit out for days, weeks, or even months, resulting in more mold infestation. Mold can cause respiratory and other health problems, especially for those with allergies.
- **Air quality:** All that clutter results in tons of dust, odors and ammonia from decaying waste products. These can cause serious air quality issues in the hoarder's home, producing respiratory problems in both people and pets.

- **Structural integrity:** Over time, hoarding can cause structural damage to the building itself due to the great weight and uneven distribution of too much stuff. Floors and load-bearing parts of a house, meant to support only a certain amount of weight, may buckle or even collapse under the strain.

Hoarding clean-up procedures

Another reason for not trying to clean up after a hoarder is that you may lack the experience, expertise and resources of a professional cleaning company that can perform the job efficiently and safely. Here's how our company tackles this difficult task:

- **We ensure safety** – Our workers must wear protective suits (PPE), which include disposable gloves and face masks, to protect themselves against bacteria and diseases. We also keep a fire extinguisher and a first-aid kit on hand.
- **We stock all needed cleaning supplies** – Everything from heavy duty tools, trash bags, boxes, buckets, universal cleaning agents, heavy duty disinfectants, etc.
- **We set up a staging area and dumpster** – An open space, such as a yard, is used to temporarily place contents pulled from the home. A large dumpster is brought in to dispose of the debris.
- **We strategically declutter the home** – When the

staging area is ready, we begin in the room nearest the closest exit to be able to escape quickly in case of emergency. The trash and clutter from each room is removed from top to bottom.

- **We sort the contents** – Local regulations are followed when handling items that can't go directly into the garbage (like paints or explosives). Then, trash and debris is bagged and placed in the dumpster. Salvageable items are sorted into items to keep and to donate.
- **We filter the air** – Air filtration fans are set up through the job site to clean the air and reduce the amount of dust while the technicians are working.
- **We repair and clean the home** – Once the entire structure is free of clutter, we assist with any needed repairs, including water, fire and mold damage. Meanwhile, all salvageable contents are cleaned and disinfected.

11. What Cold Weather Means for Viruses

Every year in springtime, cases of influenza drop dramatically in the United States. People are less cooped up and some flu strains die quickly in sunny, humid weather. In 2020 when COVID-19 hit in late winter, there was the hope that it too would dissipate with warmer and sunnier conditions. Unfortunately, that was not the case with this particular virus. So, what can you expect when cold weather is on the way?

Scientists remain divided on why winter is flu season in the Northern Hemisphere, but one of the most popular hypotheses is the increased time spent in sealed indoor environments. Another is a lack of sunlight, which compromises the immune system due to a lack of vitamin D. Viruses may also spread for these reasons.

Cold weather makes people stay indoors where it's more difficult to socially distance. As the pandemic continues, people are beginning to get complacent about meeting in large groups, which has increased the reach of the virus. In addition, the holidays, where people enjoy getting together with family and friends, may well exacerbate the problem.

Another issue is that cold air typically means dry air and, to be comfortable, people tend to turn up the heat which further dries out their homes. Why is this a concern? In cold temperatures our mucous membrane dries out, making it much harder for the nose to filter pathogens. When airways are dry, it allows the virus to have easier access to the body.

A study published in the journal Transboundary and Emerging Diseases found that the number of COVID-19 cases increased as the air became drier and the humidity level dropped. "There is growing evidence that climatic factors could influence the evolution of the current COVID-19 pandemic," the authors stated. "Overall, a decrease in relative humidity of one per cent was associated with an increase in cases of seven to eight per cent."

Temperature and relative humidity can affect coronavirus transmission as the virus can survive longer at lower temperatures, the authors said. The virus can also stay "suspended in the air" longer at lower humidity, they claimed.

What can you do to protect yourself?

Get a seasonal flu shot because it's possible to get viruses at the same time. Get immunized for viral outbreaks if immunizations are available.

- Get good sleep, don't let your body get run down
- Stay hydrated
- Eat healthily
- Keep stress in check
- Wash your hands regularly
- Increase ventilation
- Use a humidifier during cold months
- To help keep mucous membranes moist, regularly use a drug-free saline nasal spray
- Wear a mask
- Practice social distancing (six feet or more)

ABOUT THE AUTHORS

Nasutsa Mabwa
President, Restoration By Simons

Nasutsa Mabwa is President of Restoration By Simons, a MBE/WBE certified firm with the City of Chicago and the State of Illinois. Nasutsa brings an extensive background of commercial real estate development to Restoration By Simons. She is focused upon building the commercial and residential side of property restoration and construction business by nurturing and developing key real estate industry relationships.

For all her achievements and involvement, Nasutsa was awarded the Women in Real Estate Bright Horizon Award in 2008 and named one of Crain's Chicago Business's "40 Under 40 Class" of 2010. She is a 2015 Goldman Sachs 10,000 Small Businesses Graduate, and a 2015 Chicago Anchors For a Strong Economy/World Business Chicago Program Graduate. The firm is a SB100 Best of Small Business Award Winner 2021, Bronze Stevie® Award in the Female Entrepreneur of the Year category in the 18th annual Stevie Awards for Women in Business, recipient of the 2020 Better Business Bureau's Torch Award for Marketplace Ethics and the recipient of the 2020 Skokie Business of the Year Award, Honorable Mention Category.

Nasutsa previously served as a Senior Project Manager for McCaffery Interests, a real estate development firm. At McCaffery, she managed the Lakeside Development, a 600-acre mixed-use community on Chicago's southeast side. Before joining McCaffery, Nasutsa worked for the City of Chicago as an Urban Planner and Director.

Currently, Nasutsa is the President of the Board of Directors for The Evanston Chamber of Commerce. Nasutsa also was honored by the Daily Herald Business Ledger in their C-Suite Awards Ceremony, 2020, and as an Influential Women in Business 2017 by the Daily Herald Business Ledger and an Influential Woman in Business in 2018 by the Chicago Business Journal.

Nasutsa holds two advanced degrees: a master's degree in Urban Planning and Policy from the University of Illinois-Chicago and an MBA with a real estate development concentration from Roosevelt University.

ABOUT THE AUTHORS

Sam Simon

Sam Simon, Managing Director, Restoration By Simons

Email: sam@servicemaster-rbs.com

Sam Simon is the Managing Director of Restoration By Simons and has earned the highly coveted title of IICRC Master Restorer. Sam oversees the technician crews, restoration project management, sub-contractors, fleet and equipment, and works with insurance adjusters on large claim losses. Sam has over 15 years of experience in the restoration industry and is certified in water damage cleanup and restoration, fire and smoke damage restoration, mold remediation, carpet and upholstery, health services, advanced drying, odor mitigation by the IICRC and EPA Lead Renovator for Lead Safety Certification.

Prior to running operations at Restoration By Simons, Sam worked with a Chicago area restoration franchise for five years, learning the industry from soup to nuts, launching the ServiceMaster Clean service line, managing the company's marketing department and managing restoration projects.

Sam has a background in broadcast journalism working as a producer for WTTW Channel 11, producing and directing public television interstitials and spots. Before WTTW 11, Sam was a freelancer for ESPN, Fox Sports and the PGA Tour, just to name a few, and toured with bands and popular television shows such as Van Halen and Dancing With the Stars. Sam resides in Evanston, IL with his wife and two children.

ACKNOWLEDGEMENTS

Writing and compiling the information in this book was no easy task. It took many hours of work, research and fact checking. Without the help of numerous people in our industry, friends and family, this book would not be possible. Therefore, we would like to thank the following people personally and individually for their contributions, whether inspiration or knowledge, to the creation of this book.

Nasutsa's Acknowledgements

This project would not have been possible without the support of so many. Throughout our journey, we have grown personally and professionally. I would like to thank my best friend, husband, and business co-pilot, Sam, for his unwavering trust, creative energy and relentless confidence in me to succeed as a woman and minority in the restoration industry.

I thank Jacqueline Camacho, JJR Marketing, Fig Media, for her crucial motivational encouragement and support of our vision. From the first time we spoke I knew you were magnificent!

I thank the following people for helping me in business:

Dan McCaffery, my first professional mentor and sponsor to the real business world.

Jeff Owen, for his kindness and essential business legal advice.

Nicolas Mengin, our gregarious and steadfast business advisor.

Joseph Williams, for always making himself available to brainstorm through a variety of business opportunities.

Angela Valvanis, for introducing me to the Evanston Chamber of Commerce and to her vast network of business people, thank you.

Neda Howell, for her everlasting positivity and calming presence in our workspace, thank you, dear sister.

To my family – because it really does take a village:

I thank my late parents, Joseph and Eileen Mabwa, for their firm love and guiding hands to push me to my fullest girl power potential.

I thank my foster parents, Hubert and Gisela Mengin, who patiently nurtured and sheltered me as a young girl, providing stability and positive direction, merci. I would not be where I am without your care.

To my three siblings, we've always shared a close bond that I've been grateful for:

Thank you to my older sister, the ever-wise Kerensa Mabwa-Childress who raised me and has always looked out for me spiritually and holistically.

Thank you to my strong brother, the warrior Ojiambo Mabwa, departed from us too soon, but always remembered.

Thank you to my brother Namanjaba Mabwa, my "younger male twin" for his constant friendship, dance moves and endless humor.

Thank you dearest Aunt Rose for helping me to grow up with poise and grace, asante sana.

Thank you to Aunt Marcella for nurturing my firstborn, asante sana.

Sam's Acknowledgements

I begin by thanking God. Alpha and Omega, for all my direction and choices. You have blessed me in life.

Thanks to my business partner, my best friend, my dear wife and co-author, Nasutsa. I can't ask for a better partner in life, in family and in business. You are one heck of a lady, and a wonderful leader.

Thank you to Pete Duncanson - CMRS, MWR, WFR, MTC. A giant of a person, both literally and figuratively, in the restoration industry. His knowledge, compassion and sense of humor has all been an inspiration for me. I've trained with him on almost every topic in residential and commercial restoration. He is truly my sensei.

Thank you to my colleagues and friends in restoration:

Steve Vandenberg; ServiceMaster of San Francisco. I thank you for all your advice, guidance and friendship. You always pick up the phone when I call. A bright business man and a stellar service provider to his clients and customers in the San Francisco, CA area.

Edward Ranieri; IICRC MWR, MSR, MTC. Your insight on the business of commercial & residential restoration is astounding. You've helped me see the forest for the trees in the restoration industry. Always a phone call away, a true friend.

Kevin Wyndham; MWR, MSR, MTC, ServiceMaster by Lewis Construction, Warren, OH. Your knowledge of commercial and residential restoration is immense. You're always a phone call away if I run into complex cleaning and restoration issues. Our discussions about business and personal lives over cigars are the best. You're a true friend and supporter of my endeavors. Ohio is lucky to have you.

Kevin Kallas; ServiceMaster Kwik Restore, Cary, IL. Thank you for your advice and guidance. You've always made yourself available to me when I have questions. I appreciate your time and willingness to discuss things. Let's grab a burger!

- You are my friends, confidantes and guru's. I thank you from the bottom of my heart.

Thank you to my family:

My mom, Olivia! A guiding hand and staunch supporter of all I do. I love you mom.

Neda Howell, our office therapist, our spiritual leader and my kid sister.

My sisters, Noelle and Suzanne. Thanks for your support, always! The uphill climb is always easier, when I know you've got my back.

To my late dad. My first teacher on owning small businesses. He toiled for years in his apartment building, restaurant and grocery store. I started working in our businesses when I was just seven years old. I've been a businessperson in some form or another most of my life.

Thanks to my buddies through thick and thin, Teofilo Gonzalez, Myron Alicea, Jesse Dominguez, Mark Hicks, Daniel Hernandez and Jorge Diaz.

To all the negative people I've encountered along the way, the people who put obstacles in my way– THANK YOU. I use you as the steps to reach the top. You are my ladder; and I'll continue to climb.